D0253610

Ted Hughes'
Tales from Ovid
adapted by
Tim Supple and Simon Reade

other stage adaptations

GRIMM TALES
adapted by Carol Ann Duffy
dramatized by Tim Supple

MORE GRIMM TALES
adapted by Carol Ann Duffy
dramatized by the Young Vic Company

SALMAN RUSHDIE'S
HAROUN AND THE SEA OF STORIES
adapted by Tim Supple and David Tushingham

TED HUGHES'

Tales from Ovid

adapted by
Tim Supple and Simon Reade

faber and faber

First published in 1999
by Faber and Faber Limited
3 Queen Square, London WC1N 3AU

Published in the United States by Faber and Faber Inc.
a division of Farrar, Straus and Giroux Inc., New York

Typeset by Country Setting, Kingsdown, Kent CT14 8ES
Printed in England by Mackays of Chatham plc, Chatham, Kent

A CIP record for this book is available from the British Library

ISBN 0–571–20225–X

4 6 8 10 9 7 5

in memoriam
Ted Hughes

Contents

Notes on the Adaptation

Our selection of Ted Hughes' poems and our order of
playing are purposeful but not immovable.

We have adapted the piece to be devised by the
original ensemble of six women, five men and three
musician performers.

Our casting, determined by the people cast in the
original production, followed this pattern:

Actor A	Tiresias, Cinyras, Pandion, Tmolus
Actor B	Jupiter, Executioner, Apollo
Actor C	Man in 'Narcissus', Pentheus, Midas
Actor D	Narcissus, Acoetes, Pan, Tereus
Actor E	Bacchus, Hermaphroditus, Itys, Barber
Actress A	Agave, Minerva, Nurse
Actress B	Juno
Actress C	Arachne, Story-Teller
Actress D	Semele, Procne
Actress E	Echo, Philomela
Actress F	Myrrha, Salmacis

Where a character appears in brackets – e.g. (**Jupiter**) –
it denotes either:

– indirect speech in the poem has been put into direct
speech in the script, or
– a suggestion to ascribe that part of the tale to that
character.

The parentheses acknowledge that it isn't necessarily a
fixed decision.

Otherwise what a character says in the script is what
they say in the poems.

In the Ted Hughes poems, the tales of 'Myrrha' and 'Tereus and Philomela' are told by a character who speaks directly in their tale – in 'Myrrha': 'The story I am now going to tell you / Is so horrible' etc; in 'Tereus and Philomela': 'I can hardly bear to think about it, / Let alone believe it'. We have made 'Myrrha' the responsibility of a female Chorus, led by Juno, 'Tereus and Philomela' the responsibility of a Story-Teller.

Key figures such as Juno, Jupiter, Tiresias and Bacchus also link the narratives.

Elsewhere, characters narrate appropriate portions of the tales in which they appear.

Square brackets [ ] indicate a stage direction taken directly from the verse description on the whole.

As far as possible, we have attempted to retain the verse forms chosen by Ted Hughes for each tale. The equivalent of stanza breaks are therefore indicated by a larger gap than the gap between characters' speeches.

Very occasionally we have added the odd word for dramatic effect: Juno's 'So . . . And' in 'Semele' for example.

Words in Latin are Ovid's. We provide a translation for reference where appropriate. The words are always sung: by nymphs lamenting the death of their brother, Narcissus, or when they humour Pan; by the women of Thebes blessing Bacchus; or by the Singer, a story-telling alter-ego we have created from the numerous references to songs, blessings, rituals of honour.

Otherwise, the vast majority of words are by Ted Hughes.

Simon Reade, Tim Supple,
Spring 1999

Introduction

BY TED HUGHES

from his original collection *Tales from Ovid:
Twenty-four Passages from the 'Metamorphoses'*
(published by Faber and Faber, 1997)

Ovid was born the year after the death of Julius Caesar
and flourished in the Rome of Augustus. He completed
the *Metamorphoses* around the time of the birth of Christ,
was later banished for some unknown offence against the
Emperor, and spent the last ten years of his life in exile at
Tomis on the Black Sea.

In its length and metre, the *Metamorphoses* resembles
an epic. But the opening lines describe the very different
kind of poem that Ovid set out to write: an account of
how from the beginning of the world right down to his
own time bodies had been magically changed, by the
power of the gods, into other bodies.

This licensed him to take a wide sweep through the
teeming underworld or overworld of Romanised Greek
myth and legend. The right man had met the right
material at the right moment. The *Metamorphoses* was a
success in its own day. During the Middle Ages throughout the Christian West it became the most popular work
from the Classical era, a source-book of imagery and
situations for artists, poets and the life of high culture.
It entered English poetry at a fountainhead, as one of
Chaucer's favourite books, which he plundered openly,
sometimes – as with the tale of Pyramus and Thisbe – in
quite close translation. A little later, it played an even
more dynamic role for Shakespeare's generation – and
perhaps for Shakespeare in particular. The 'sweet, witty

soul' of Ovid was said to live again in him. But perhaps Shakespeare's closest affinity lay not so much in the sweet, witty Ovidian facility for 'sniffing out the odoriferous flowers of fancy', as one of his characters put it, nor in his aptitude for lifting images or even whole passages nearly verbatim, nor in drawing from two stories in the *Metamorphoses* his own best-seller, the seminal long poem *Venus and Adonis*. A more crucial connection, maybe, can be found in their common taste for a tortured subjectivity and catastrophic extremes of passion that border on the grotesque. In this vein, Shakespeare's most Ovidian work was his first – *Titus Andronicus*. Thirty or so dramas later in *Cymbeline*, his mild and blameless heroine Imogen – whom her beloved husband will try to murder, whom her loathed stepbrother will try to rape – chooses for her bedtime reading Ovid's shocking tale of Tereus and Philomela.

Different aspects of the poem continued to fascinate Western culture, saturating literature and art. And by now, many of the stories seem inseparable from our unconscious imaginative life.

Why the world should have so clasped Ovid's versions of these myths and tales to its bosom is a mystery. As a guide to the historic, original forms of the myths, Ovid is of little use. His attitude to his material is like that of the many later poets who have adapted what he presents. He too is an adaptor. He takes up only those tales which catch his fancy, and engages with each one no further than it liberates his own creative zest. Of those he does take up – about two hundred and fifty in all – he gives his full attention to only a proportion, sketching the others more briefly in ornamental digressions or cramming them as clusters of foreshortened portraits into some eddy of his unfurling drift.

Myths and fantastic legends, wonder-tales about the embroilment of the natural human world with the supernatural, obviously held a quite special attraction for him – as they have done for most people throughout history. But this aspect of his material, though it is usually dominant, does not altogether explain his addictive appeal for generations of imaginative artists. Nor does his urbane, cavalier lightness of touch, or the swiftness and filmic economy of his narrative, or the playful philosophical breadth of his detachment, his readiness to entertain every possibility, his strange yoking of incompatible moods. All these qualities are there, with many more, and all are important. But perhaps what has gone deepest into his long succession of readers, and brought him so intimately into the life of art, is what he shared with Shakespeare. Above all, Ovid was interested in passion. Or rather, in what a passion feels like to the one possessed by it. Not just ordinary passion either, but human passion *in extremis* – passion where it combusts, or levitates, or mutates into an experience of the supernatural.

This is the current he divines and follows in each of his tales – the current of human passion. He adapts each myth to this theme. Where details or complexities of the traditional story encumber or diffuse his theme, he simply omits them. He must have known the full myth of Venus and Adonis, in which the Goddess of Love and her opposite in the underworld, the Goddess of Death, quarrel for possession of the baby Adonis, and in which the Boar has multiple identities, and where the whole sequence of events completes the annual cycle of the sacrificed god. But all Ovid wants is the story of hopelessly besotted and doomed love in the most intense form imaginable – as suffered by the love-goddess herself.

The act of metamorphosis, which at some point touches each of the tales, operates as the symbolic guarantee that the passion has become mythic, has achieved the unendurable intensity that lifts the whole episode onto the supernatural or divine plane. Sometimes this happens because

xiii

mortals tangle with gods, sometimes because mortal
passion makes the breakthrough by sheer excess, without
divine intervention – as in the tale of Tereus and Philomela.
But in every case, to a greater or lesser degree, Ovid
locates and captures the peculiar frisson of that event,
where the all-too-human victim stumbles out into the
mythic arena and is transformed.

However impossible these intensities might seem to be
on one level, on another, apparently more significant level
Ovid renders them with compelling psychological truth
and force. In his earlier books, preoccupied with erotic
love, he had been a sophisticated entertainer. Perhaps here
too in the *Metamorphoses* he set out simply to entertain.
But something else joined in, something emerging from the
very nature of his materials yet belonging to that unique
moment in history – the moment of the birth of Christ
within the Roman Empire. The Greek/Roman pantheon
had fallen in on men's heads. The obsolete paraphernalia
of the old official religion were lying in heaps, like old
masks in the lumber room of a theatre, and new ones had
not yet arrived. The mythic plane, so to speak, had been
defrocked. At the same time, perhaps one could say as a
result, the Empire was flooded with ecstatic cults. For all
its Augustan stability, it was at sea in hysteria and despair,
at one extreme wallowing in the bottomless appetites and
sufferings of the gladiatorial arena, and at the other
searching higher and higher for a spiritual transcendence –
which eventually did take form, on the crucifix. The
tension between these extremes, and occasionally their
collision, can be felt in these tales. They establish a rough
register of what it feels like to live in the psychological
gulf that opens at the end of an era. Among everything
else that we see in them, we certainly recognise this.

Tales from Ovid (7 AD)

BY TED HUGHES (1997)
ADAPTATION: TIM SUPPLE AND SIMON READE (1999)

exceptional tales
of extraordinary transformation
spun from ancient history,
from Greek myth and Roman folklore,
from the stories of Babylon and Eastern civilization
and from pagan legend,
as related by the Latin poet Ovid
in the 'Metamorphoses'
two thousand years ago
and retold by Ted Hughes
at the end of the twentieth century

The world première of *Tales from Ovid* was at the Royal Shakespeare Company's Swan Theatre, Stratford-upon-Avon, on 9 April 1999.

Ensemble:
Sam Dastor **Tiresias, Cinyras, Pandion, Tmolus**
Andrew Dennis **Jupiter, Executioner, Apollo**
Antony Byrne **Man in 'Narcissus', Pentheus, Midas**
Mark Bonnar **Narcissus, Acoetes, Pan, Tereus**
Fergus O'Donnell **Bacchus, Hermaphroditus, Itys, Barber**
Cherry Morris **Agave, Minerva, Nurse**
Susannah Elliot-Knight **Juno**
Rebecca Lenkiewicz **Arachne, Story-Teller**
Alison Reid **Semele, Procne**
Sarah Walton **Echo, Philomela**
Sirine Saba **Myrrha, Salmacis**
Sylvia Hallett **Singer, Musician**
Jan Hendrickse **Musician**
James Jones **Musician**

Other parts played by members of the ensemble.
The production was devised by the ensemble.

Director Tim Supple
Designer and Co-Director Melly Still
Dramaturg Simon Reade
Music and Sound Adrian Lee
Lighting Designer Paule Constable
Sound Co-Designer Andrea J. Cox
Music Director (performances) Sylvia Hallett
Music Director (rehearsals) Adrian Lee
Assistant Director Timothy Sheader
Company Voice Work Andrew Wade
Production Manager Stuart Gibbons
Costume Supervisor Jo Staples
Stage Manager Jondon

Deputy Stage Manager Simon Sinfield
Assistant Stage Manager Richard Clayton

The composer wishes to thank Sylvia Hallett, Jan Hendrickse, Simon Limbrick (percussion repetiteur, rehearsals) and James Jones for their input into musical arrangements.

Tales from Ovid

PART ONE

Metamorphosis

(Singer)

    In nova fert animus mutates dicere formas
    corpora:
    Now I am ready to tell how bodies are changed
    Into different bodies.

    Some are transformed just once
    And live their whole lives after in that shape.
    Others have a facility
    For changing themselves as they please.

    Now am I ready to tell how bodies are changed
    Into different bodies:
    In nova fert animus mutates dicere formas
    corpora.

TIRESIAS

(Jupiter)
    One time, Jupiter, happy to be idle,
    Swept the cosmic mystery aside
    And draining another goblet of ambrosia
    Teased Juno,

(Juno)
               who drowsed in bliss beside him.

Jupiter
    This love of male and female is a strange business.
    Fifty-fifty investment in the madness,
    Yet she ends up with nine-tenths of the pleasure.

Juno
            A man might think so.
    It needs more than a mushroom in your cup
    To wake a wisdom that can fathom which
    Enjoys the deeper pleasure, man or woman.
    It needs the solid knowledge of a soul
    Who having lived and loved in woman's body
    Has also lived and loved in the body of a man.

Jupiter [*laughing*]
    We have the answer.
    There is a fellow called Tiresias.
    Strolling to watch the birds and hear the bees
    He came across two serpents copulating.
    He took the opportunity to kill
    Both with a single blow, but merely hurt them –
    And found himself transformed into a woman.

After the seventh year of womanhood,
Strolling to ponder on what women ponder
She saw in that same place the same two serpents
Knotted as before in copulation.

Tiresias (*woman*)
If your pain can still change your attacker
Just as you once changed me, then change me back.

Jupiter
She hit the couple with a handy stick,

And there he stood as male as any man.

Juno
He'll explain why you are
Slave to your irresistible addiction
While the poor nymphs you force to share it with you
Do all they can to shun it.

Jupiter (*to Tiresias*)
In their act of love
Who takes the greater pleasure, man or woman?

Tiresias
Woman takes nine-tenths.

(Juno)
Juno was so angry –

(Jupiter)
                             angrier
Than is easily understandable –

(Juno)
She struck Tiresias

(Jupiter)
                         and blinded him.

Juno
You've seen your last pretty snake, for ever.

Jupiter [*consoling Tiresias*]
That same blow
Has opened your inner eye, like a nightscope. See:

The secrets of the future – they are yours.

(Tiresias)
When the prophetic vision awoke
Behind the blind eyes of Tiresias
And stared into the future,

The first to test how deeply he saw
And how lucidly
Was Liriope, a swarthy nymph of the fountain.

She was swept off her feet by the river Cephisus
Who rolled her into the bed of a dark pool
Then cast her up on the shingle, pregnant.

The boy she bore, even in his cradle,
Had a beauty that broke hearts.
She named the child

(Liriope)
                Narcissus.

(Woman)
                    Gossips

Came to Tiresias:

(Man)
              Can the boy live long
With such perfect beauty?

Tiresias
Yes, unless he learns to know himself.

(Man)

    All regarded these words as a riddle –
    Till time solved them with a strange madness.
    A stranger death completed the explanation.

(Tiresias)

    In his sixteenth year Narcissus,
    Still a slender boy but already a man,
    Infatuated many. His beauty had flowered,

(Man)

    But something glassy about it, a pride,
    Kept all his admirers at a distance.
    None dared be familiar, let alone touch him.

(Narcissus)

    A day came, out on the mountain
    Narcissus was driving and netting and killing the deer

(Echo)

    When Echo saw him.

(Tiresias)

    Echo who cannot be silent
    When another speaks. Echo who cannot
    Speak at all
    Unless another has spoken.
    Echo, who always answers back.

(Echo)

    The moment Echo saw Narcissus

She was in love. She followed him
Like a starving wolf
Following a stag too strong to be tackled.
She almost burst
With longing to call out to him and somehow
Let him know what she felt.

(Tiresias)
But she had to wait
For some other to speak
So she could snatch their last words
With whatever sense they might lend her.

It so happened, Narcissus
Had strayed apart
From his companions.

Narcissus
Where are you?
I'm here.

Echo [*catching at the syllables as if they are precious*]
I'm here, I'm here, I'm here, I'm here.

Narcissus (*looking around wildly*)
I'll stay here.
You come to me.

Echo
Come to me,
To me, to me, to me.

[*Narcissus stands baffled
whether to stay or go.
He begins to run.*]

Narcissus
Stay there.

Echo (*weeping*)
Stay there,
Stay there, stay there, stay there.

[*Narcissus stops and listens.*]

Narcissus [*more quietly*]
Let's meet halfway. Come.

Echo (*eagerly*)
Come come come come.

[*Echo emerges from the undergrowth,
her expression pleading,
her arms raised to embrace him –
Narcissus turns and runs.*]

Narcissus
No, no, I would sooner be dead
Than let you touch me.

Echo [*collapsing in sobs, voice lurching*]
Touch me, touch me, touch me, touch me.

(Tiresias)
Echo moped under the leaves.
Humiliated, she hid
In the deep woods.

(Echo)
But love was fixed in her body
Like a barbed arrow. There it festered
With his rejection. Sleeplessly
She brooded over the pain,
Wasting away as she suffered,
The petal of her beauty
Fading and shrivelling, falling from her –

Leaving her voice and bones.

(Tiresias)
　　Her bones, they say, turned
　　Into stone, sinking into the humus.
　　Her voice roamed off by itself,
　　Unseen in the forest, unseen
　　On the empty mountainside –
　　Though all could hear it
　　Living the only life left to Echo.

(Man)
　　Narcissus had rebuffed her adoration
　　As he had the passionate attentions
　　Of many another nymph of the wilderness –
　　And many another man.

Man [*lifting his hands to heaven*]
　　Let Narcissus love and suffer
　　As he has made us suffer.
　　Let him, like us, love and know it is hopeless.
　　And let him, like Echo, perish of anguish.

(Tiresias)
　　Nemesis, the corrector,
　　Heard this prayer and granted it.

　　There is a pool of perfect water.
　　No shepherd had ever driven sheep
　　To trample the margins. No cattle
　　Had slobbered their muzzles in it
　　And befouled it. No wild beast
　　Had ever dashed through it.
　　No bird had ever paddled there preening and bathing.
　　Only surrounding grasses drank its moisture

And though the arching trees kept it cool
No twigs rotted in it, and no leaves.

(**Narcissus**)
Weary with hunting and the hot sun
Narcissus found this pool.

[*Narcissus gratefully stretches out full length,*
cups his hands in the clear cold water
and drinks.]

                                        As he drank
A strange new thirst, a craving, unfamiliar,
Entered his body with the water,
And entered his eyes
With the reflection in the limpid mirror.
He could not believe the beauty
Of those eyes that gazed into his own.
As the taste of water flooded him
So did love.

[*Narcissus plunges his arms deep to embrace*
the one who vanishes in the agitated water.
Again and again he kisses
the lips that seem to be rising to kiss his lips
but dissolve as he kisses them into a soft splash
    and ripples.
He does not comprehend.
He becomes excited by it.]

He could not go.
He wanted neither to eat nor sleep.
Only to lie there.

[*Narcissus lies there –*
gazing.
He sits up, lifts his arms, calls to the forest.]

Narcissus

                    You trees,
Was there ever a love
As cruel as mine is to me?
Was there ever a love
As futureless as mine?
What I love is untouchable.
We are kept apart
Neither by seas nor mountains
Nor the locked-up gates of cities.
Nothing at all comes between us –
Only the skin of water.

Who are you? Come out. Come up
Onto the land. I never saw beauty
To compare with yours.

[*He lunges once more.*]

It cannot be my ugliness
Or my age that repels you
If all the nymphs are so crazy about me.
I stretch my arms to you, you stretch yours
As eagerly to me. You laugh when I laugh.
When I tell you my love I see your lips
Seeming to tell me yours – though I cannot hear it.

You are me.
I am in love with myself.
I torture myself. What am I doing –
Loving or being loved?
What can my courtship gain?
What I want, I am.

This impotent grief
Is taking my strength
And my life.
My beauty is in full bloom –
But I am a cut flower.
Let death come quickly –
Carry me off
Where this pain
Can never follow.
The one I loved should be let live –
He should live on after me, blameless.
But when I go – both go.

(Tiresias)
    Then Narcissus wept into the pool
    And his image blurred.

(Narcissus)
                        Don't leave me
    If I cannot touch you at least let me see you.

(Tiresias)
    He ripped off his shirt
    And beat his bare chest with white fists.
    The skin flushed under the blows.

(Narcissus)
    When Narcissus saw this
    In the image returned to perfection
    Where the pool had calmed
    It was too much for him.

(Tiresias)
    Like wax near the flame,
    Or like the hoar-frost
    Where the first ray of the morning sun
    Creeps across it,
    He melted – consumed

By his love.
He disappeared from his own eyes.

Narcissus
Alas!

Voice of Echo (*weeping*)
Alas.

Narcissus (*to his reflection*)
Farewell you incomparable boy,
I have loved you in vain.

Voice of Echo [*sorrowful*]
I have loved you in vain.

Narcissus
Farewell.

Voice of Echo
Farewell.

[*The nymphs sing a lament –
the voice of Echo repeats the refrain.*]

(**Nymphs**) [*singing*]
ille caput viridi fessum submisit in herba,
lumina mors clausit domini mirantia formam:
tum quoque se, postquam est inferna sede receptus,
in Stygia spectabat aqua.

(**Voice of Echo**) [*singing*]
in Stygia spectabat aqua
    spectabat aqua

[*Hughes' translation:*
He pillowed his head on the grass.
So finally death
Closed the eyes that had loved
    themselves too much.

When he entered the Land of the Dead
Narcissus could not resist it –
He ran straight to the banks of the Styx
And gazed down at the smear of his shadow
Trembling on the fearful current]

[*Men arrive with crackling torches.*]

(**Man**)
When men came with timber
To build a pyre,
No corpse could be found.
But there, in the pressed grass where he had perished,
A tall flower stood unbroken –
Bowed, a ruff of white petals
Round a dainty bugle centre
Yellow as egg yolk.

(**Tiresias**)
Yes, it was this quiet woodland flower
Trumpeted the fame of Tiresias
Throughout Achaia.

[*The nymphs' lament transforms into a fanfare
of fame.*]

(Juno)
>Juno was incensed when she learned it:
>Jove had impregnated Semele.
>
>[*Curses*
>*come bursting out of her throat, but she swallows them*
>*hissing*:]

Juno

>   Anger is lost on Jupiter. Only

>Let me get my hands on that woman.
>As sure as I am Juno, the Queen of Heaven,
>As sure as I grasp the sceptre
>And am Jove's wife and sister –
>As sure as I am at the very least his sister –

>I shall destroy that whore.
>Let others excuse her. They say she takes nothing
>If this taste of his love is all she takes.
>They say she's no more trespassed on my marriage
>Than a cloud-shadow crossing a mountain.

>They should know the fact:
>His brat is in her womb.
>Jupiter's own child – out of her womb!

>More than I ever gave him.
>A splendid-looking woman –
>And so pleased with herself, to be so splendid.

Her pleasure is a delusion.
Her beauty comes at a cost, she will find.

I am not the daughter of Saturn
If she does not stumble very soon
Headlong into hell's horrible river,
Pushed there and shoved under
By the loving caresses of none other
Than her darling, the high god Jupiter.

(Juno)
Juno rose
Like a puff of smoke from a volcano.
In a globe of whirling light
She arrived at the home of Semele.

(Semele)
Semele
Looked up at the shadow. There,
Standing on the threshold, a gummy old woman –

(Juno)
The very double of Beroe,

Semele's old nurse from Epidaurus.

(Semele)
Semele recognised and welcomed
Her old nurse.

(Juno)
                    She never doubted a moment.
Their gossiping began to circle,
Touching at Semele's swollen belly.

Juno (Beroe) [*sighing*]
    Ah, I pray you are right,
    I pray that Jupiter is the sire, as you say –

    You wouldn't be the first simple virgin
    To hear an unscrupulous seducer
    Reveal his greatest secret – that he is a god.
    That child
    Is going to demand real proof.

    Jupiter should give you real proof
    That he is himself. Ask him to face you
    Naked as for Juno in heaven,
    In all his omnipotence and glory,
    The great god of the triple-headed sceptre.

(Juno)
    Listening to the twisty words of Juno
    Semele heard
    Only the purest wisdom.
    So:

    [*enter Jupiter*]

(Semele)
    Divine lover! Give me a love gift –
    A gift I will name only if it is granted.

Jupiter [*smiling*]
    Whatever you want – name it,
    You shall have it.

(Juno)
                    And:

Jupiter

                    I swear
On the terror who holds all heaven in awe –
The god of hell's river – you shall have it.

[*Semele is triumphant.*]

Semele

              I want to see you
Exactly as Juno sees you when she opens
Her arms and body to you. As if I were Juno,
Come to me naked – in your divine form.

[*Too late*

*Jupiter guesses what she is asking
and tries to gag her
with his hand. He groans.*]

(Juno)

His oath could no more be retracted
Than her words could be unuttered.
Yes, God wept a little
Gathering the foggy clouds around him
As he withdrew into heaven.

Now he piled above him the purple
Topheavy thunderclouds
Churning with tornadoes
And inescapable bolts of lightning.

(Jupiter)

Yet he did what he could to insulate

And filter
The nuclear blast
Of his naked impact.

(Juno)
Arrayed in this fashion
Jove came to the house of Semele.

*[Jupiter enters Semele's bedchamber,
but as he bends over
to kiss her:]*

(Semele)
Her eyes open wide, see him
And burst into flame.
Then her whole body lights up
With the glare
That explodes the lamp –

(Jupiter)
In that splinter of a second,
Before her blazing shape
Became a silhouette of sooty ashes,
The foetus was snatched from her womb.

(Bacchus)
If this is a true story,

That babe was then inserted into Jove's thigh,
To be born, at full term, not from his mother
But from his father – reborn. Son of the father.
And this was the twice-born god – the god Bacchus.

(Tiresias)
So the fame of the blind
Seer Tiresias
Flared up in all the Greek cities.
Only Pentheus, King of Thebes,
Laughed at the old man's prophecies.

Pentheus
Infill for empty skulls,
Dreams,
Which this methane-mouth
Tells us are the dark manifesto
Of the corrector,
In fact are corpse-lights, the ignes fatui,
Miasma from the long-drop
And fermenting pit
Of what we don't want, don't need,
And have dumped.
They rise from the lower bowel. And lower.

[*He laughs.*]

Tiresias
If only you, like me, had managed
To get rid of your two eyes
That so sharply
Supervise everything and see nothing.
Then you would not have to watch
What Bacchus will do to you.
These dreams, that you miscall ridiculous
And that attract your derision,
These dreams
Have shown me this new god, son of Semele,

And they have shown me a preview, in full colour,
Of a banquet
Bacchus will hold for you, Pentheus,
At which you will be not only guest of honour
But the food and drink. Think of it.
Your expensive coiffeur
With your face wrapped in it
Wrenched off like a cork, at the neck,
Your blood
Poured out over your mothers and sisters,
Your pedigree carcase
Ripped by unthinking fingers
Into portions.
All this, Pentheus, as clear as if
It had already happened, I saw
In a silly dream
Which this new god, outlawed by you,
Gave to me on a street corner.
Gave to me – for me to give to you.
What can it mean?

[*Pentheus roars
and kicks the old blind man
like a stray befouling dog
from his palazzo.*]

[*The Bacchus revels begin.*]

(Tiresias)
    The god has come.
    The city pours
    Its entire population into the frenzy:

(All)
    Children, teachers, labourers, bankers,

Mothers, grandmothers, merchants, agents,
Prostitutes, politicians, police,
Scavengers, accountants, lawyers, burglars,
Builders, layabouts, tradesmen, con-men,
Scoundrels, tax-collectors, academicians,
Physicians, morticians, musicians, magicians,
The idle rich, the laughing mob –

(Tiresias)
All, as if naked, anonymous, freed
Into the ecstasy,
The dementia and the delerium
Of the new god.

Pentheus screams like an elephant:

Pentheus
This is a disease –
Toads have got into the wells,
The granaries have all gone to fungus.
You forget, you Thebans,
You are the seed of the god Mars.
Remember your ancestry.
You veterans, what has happened to your hearing –
It was cured and seasoned
By the crash of weaponry and the war-cries
And the dying cries of the enemy.
How can you go capering
After a monkey stuffed with mushrooms?
How can you let yourselves be bitten
By this hopping tarantula?
You pioneers, you first settlers, heroes,
You who raised our city, stone by stone,
Out of the slime of the salt marsh,
How can you
Go rolling your eyes and waggling your fingers

After that claque of poltroons?
Remember
How often you dragged yourselves, by your teeth
  and nails,
Out of the mass graves
And the fields of massacre,
Clutching your wives and new-born:
Can a fed-back, millionfold
Amplified heartbeat
And some drunken woman's naked heel tossed over
  your heads
Bounce you out of your wits –
Like bobbing unborn babies?
Iron warriors, menhirs of ancient manhood,
Tootling flutes
Wet as spaghetti?
And you philosophers,
Metaphysicians, where are your systems?
What happened to the great god Reason?
And to the stone table of Law?
You have become sots,
You have dunked it all, like a doughnut,
Into a mugful of junk music –
Which is actually the belly-laugh
Of this androgynous, half-titted witch.
You forget the hard face of the future
With its hungry mouth and its battle cry
That waits behind the time of plenty
Hungry for all you have,
And that massacres for amusement, for thrills.
You forget the strangers who are not friendly.
They will lift off your roofs and remove your walls
  like driftwood
And take all you have,
Leaving you hugging the burnt earth.
If Thebes has to fall

That would be better.
We could succumb to such a fate with honour.
Then our despair would resemble a noble trophy,
Our tears would be monumental.
But you have surrendered the city
Not to war's elemental chaos
And heroes harder and readier than yourselves
But to a painted boy, a butterfly face,
Swathed in glitter.
A baboon
Got up as an earring
In the ear of a jigging whore.

As for this lewd, blasphemous joke
About his birth:
Begotten by God himself,
Snatched by his father's scorched fingers
Out of the incineration of his mother,
Sodden, squirming, no bigger than a newt,
Then gestated full term
In the thigh of Almighty God –
Like a papoose
In God's scrotum –
Do you hear this fairy tale?
How can you swallow it? Bring the juggler to me.
Let me get my thumbs on that Adam's apple,
I'll pop this lie out of him, with squeals,
Like the pip of yellow
Out of a boil.
Bring him.

(Tiresias)
With the dry foam framing his lips
Pentheus sent his praetorian guard
To arrest this creature, this Bacchus,
Acclaimed as a new god.

[*The guards come back bruised and dishevelled.*]

Pentheus

They bring to Pentheus not the Bacchus he wanted
But a different prisoner:

Executioner

A priest of new rites.

[*Pentheus's glare, a white-hot branding iron,
bears down on the face of this prisoner.
With difficulty he calms
his homicidal hands.*]

Pentheus

Your death approaches
Very fast, simply because
Your friends need the warning. So: quickly:
What is your homeland, your family, and your name?
And how does it come about
That you end up here, the manikin doll
Of this ventriloquial, mesmeric,
Itinerant common fraud?

Acoetes [*fearless*]

I am Acoetes, out of Maeonia.
My parents were poor.
My father possessed neither stock
Nor ground for it to stand on.
His wealth
Was a barbed hook and the art
Of finding fish with it.
These, and the wilderness of waters,
Were his bequest to me.
But I grew weary of wading among herons.
I took to open water.
I pushed a prow out through breakers.

I stretched my cunning
Between the tiller, the sail
And the constellations.

One time,
My destination Delos, I was blown
Onto the coast of Chios.
Skill with the oars got us ashore safely.
That night we camped there. At dawn
I sent Opheltes, the bosun, with men
To find fresh water,
While I climbed a headland
To study the wind, the sky-signs, the horizons.
Everything looked promising. I returned
To the ship, recalling my crew.
'Look what we've found,' shouted Opheltes.
He shoved ahead of him a strange boy,
A little boy, beautiful as a girl.
They'd picked him up on the hillside.
Straight away they'd recognised plunder.

[*The girl-boy staggers,
mouth half open, eyelids heavy.*]

He was ready to collapse
With wine, or sleep, or both.
But I saw, I knew, by everything
About him, this boy was more than mortal.
I said to the crew: 'I do not know
Which god you have found but I am certain
This child is divine.'
Then I spoke to the boy: 'Whoever you are,
Preserve our lives in the sea, bless our voyage,
And forgive these fellows
Their rough words and their rough hands.'

'None of that rubbish,' cried Dictys. 'This boy's ours.'
The girlish boy
Was a landfall, a whole port
For these testy sailors.
'Bestial sacrilege,' I told them,
'Shall not defile this vessel
While I am master of it!'

The worst among them pretended to retch.
Lycabus. He was so reckless
He seemed to be searching everywhere
With a kind of desperation
For his own violent death.
He grabbed at my throat with his rower's fingers
And would have pitched me overboard
But I caught hold of a rope, and between my knee
And his pelvic bone
Gave his testicles the fright of their lives.
The whole crew bellowed, with one voice:

(All)

                                                  Get up
And finish what you've started!

Bacchus [*roused*]
My friends,
What was that awful noise?
Where am I? How did I get here?
Are you planning to take me somewhere?

Acoetes
Proreus found a soft voice.
'Nothing to be afraid of. You seemed lost.
We thought you'd like a lift
Where do you want to go?
Wherever you say – and we'll drop you off.'

Bacchus

    Naxos is my home. Take me there
    And many friends for life
    Will give you a welcome to remember.

Acoetes

    Those criminals
    With sudden hilarity
    Swore by the sea and all its gods to take him.
    And they urged me to get under way –
    I set the painted prow
    Towards Naxos.
    The crew, their faces,
    Their mouthings, their gestures, made it plain
    They wanted me to take the boy where they pleased,
    Very far from Naxos.
    I could not believe
    They could suppose a god could be tricked by men.
    I told them:
    'This is not only wicked – it is stupid.
    I'll have no part in it.'
    Then one of them, Aethalion,
    Shouldered me from the helm.
    'In that case,' he said, 'leave our fortunes to us.'

    As the ship heeled, the god of actors
    Went reeling off balance. He clutched the gunwhale,
    Stared at the churned swerve in the wake
    And pretended to weep.

Bacchus [*feigning wailing*]

    This is not the way home,
    The sun should be on that side. We were
    Right before. What have I done wrong?
    What is the world going to say
    If the whole crew of you
    Kidnap one small boy?

Acoetes

Those bandits laughed at his tears
And they laughed at me too, for mine.
But I swear
By the god himself –
And there is no god closer to hear me –
That the incredible
Truly now did happen.

First, the ship stops dead in the sea
As if rammed into a dry dock.
The oarsmen are amazed. They grimace
And force the blood from under their fingernails
To budge the hull or shear the rowlocks.
The sails are helpless,
Flogging in their ropes. Then suddenly ivy
Comes swarming up the oars
And tumbles in over the deck,
Coiling up the masts,
Draping the sails. And the god
Is standing there, mid-ship, crowned
With clusters of fat grapes.
He brandishes a javelin.
And around him are heaped, as if real,
The great shapes of big cats.

(Bacchus)

Then either in panic terror or godsent madness
Every man leaps up, as if for his life,
And overboard into the sea –

Acoetes

Medon was the first to go black.
His spine arched into a half-wheel, mid-air.

Lycabus gibbered at him. 'Look he's changing
Into a sea-monster – '

(Bacchus)

As his own gape widened
Backwards beneath his ears, in the long smile
Of a dolphin, and his nose flattened,
His body slicked smooth, his skin toughened.
Another was reaching up
To free the ropes from the ivy
And found he had no arms. With a howl
He somersaulted over the stern
In a high arc
Flailing the black half-moon of a dolphin-tail
That was suddenly his.
These creatures crash round the ship
Like a troupe of acrobatic dancers –
Blasting out in a fume, through their blowholes,
The sea they gulp as they frolic.

Acoetes

I was the survivor of twenty,
Shuddering with fear, barely sane.
But the god was kind.

Bacchus

Now steer towards Dia.

Acoetes

And I did so. And there I was rewarded.
I entered the priesthood of this mighty god.

[*Pause.*]

Pentheus

You have dreamed us a long dream,
With a deal of ocean bluster,
But my anger has neither slept nor cooled.

[*to Executioner*] Break this man on the rack
  elaborately.
Send him down to hell grateful
For the respite.

(Tiresias)
  So Acoetes was dragged off, and slammed
  Into a strongroom.
  But it is told:

(Executioner)
  While I readied my implements
  Of fire, pincers, choppers, and incidentals,
  To gratify Pentheus, of a sudden
  Bolts shot out of their sockets and went skittering
  Over the floors. Locks exploded
  In a scatter of components curiously fractured.
  Doors flew open untouched.
  And untouched the shackles
  Fell off Acoetes.

(Pentheus)
  Pentheus heard of this.

(Tiresias)
                  But from it
  Learned nothing. Instead, his brain temperature
  Rose a degree. Something insane
  Behind his eyes
  Tore off its straitjacket.

(Pentheus)
  He thought no more of bodyguards
  Than of jailors, warders, doctors, nurses.
  Alone he climbed Cithaeron,

(Tiresias)
    The mountain consecrated to Bacchus,

(Tiresias) *and* (Pentheus)
    Where the air
    Pounded his eardrums like mad fists

(Pentheus)
    And seemed to pound in his heart,
    And the screaming songs of the possessed
    Were like the screams of a horse, reverberating
    Inside the horse's own skull.
    He heard the unbearable howls.
    When he stumbled in his fury
    And fell on all fours,
    When he clutched the earth and felt their stamping
    Shaking the mountain beneath his fingers,
    When Pentheus
    Saw the frightened worms
    Twisting up out of their burrows
    Then the red veil came over his vision.

    [*The howls
    and ululations of the Bacchantes; the blast of the
        trumpets,
    the clash of their cymbals.*]

(Tiresias)
    Pentheus bounded into the open
    And halted –
    Utterly unprepared
    For what he had surprised.
    He stared, in a stupor,
    Into the naked mysteries.

    The first to see him,
    The first to come for him

Like a bear defending her cubs,
The first to drive her javelin into him
Was his own mother –

Agave
It's the boar that ploughed up our gardens!
I've hit it! Quickly, sisters, now we can kill it!

(Tiresias)
And the whole horde of women
Pile on top of him
Like a pack of wild dogs.

Pentheus
Bites at new words,
Strange words, words that curse himself.

Pentheus
Autone, Aunt,
Remember your darling Actaeon
Torn to rags by the hounds that loved him.
Pity me.

(Tiresias)
          The name Actaeon
Sounds to Autone like the scream of a pig
As she wrenches his right arm
Out of its socket and clean off.
While Ino, with the strength of the god,
Twists the other likewise clean off.
Pentheus lurches towards his mother.

Pentheus [sobbing]
Mother, Mother, look at me,
Recognise me, Mother!

(Tiresias)
Agave stares, she blinks, her mouth wide.

She takes her son's head between her hands
And rips it from his shoulders.
She lifts it, like a newborn baby,
Her red fingers hooked into the hair
Letting the blood splash over her face and breasts –

Agave [*screeching*]
Victory! I've done it! I did it!

(Tiresias)
Swiftly,
So swiftly
The hands of those women
Separated the King's bones and stripped them.

The lesson was not lost on Thebes.
Women made sure, thereafter,
That this sleepy child was acknowledged, was
    honoured
And made happy by all who played with him
In his ritual play,
Blessing all who blessed him.

(Women) [*singing*]
    Bacchumque Bromiumque Lyaeumque
ignigenamque satumque iterum solumque bimatrem;
    Nyseus Thyoneus
et cum Lenaeo genialis consitor uvae
Nycteliusque Eleleusque parens et Iacchus et Euhan,
et quae praeterea per Graias plurima gentes
nomina, Liber, habes. tibi enim inconsumpta iuventa est,
tu puer aeternus, tu formosissimus alto
conspiceris caelo; tibi, cum sine cornibus adstas,
virgineum caput est;
Placatus mistique adsis!

[*Translation from the opening of Book IV, Loeb edition:*
Bacchus (= *rage*) Bromius (= *noisy*) Lyaeumque
    (= *deliverer from care*)
Son of the thunderbolt, twice born, child of two
    mothers;
Nyseus (= *of Nysa, in India, connected with Bacchus'*
    infancy) Thyoneus (= *son of Thyone, Semele's new*
    name after being blasted in the skies)
Lenaeus, planter of the joy-giving vine,
Nyctelius (= *night, when Bacchanalias take place*)
    father Eleleus (= *the cries of the Bacchantes*) Iacchus
    (= *Bacchus*) and Euhan,
And all the many names besides by which you are
Known, oh Liber (= *free*), throughout the towns of
    Greece,
Yours is unending youth, eternal boyhood; you are
    the most lovely
In the lofty sky; if you stand before us without horns,
Your face is virgin-seeming.
Be with us, merciful and mild!]

(Minerva)
    Minerva, goddess of weavers,
    Had heard too much of Arachne.
    She had heard
    That the weaving of Arachne
    Equalled her own, or surpassed it.

(Arachne)
    Arachne was humbly born. Her father
    Laboured as a dyer
    Of Phocaean purple. Her mother
    Had been humbly born.

(Tiresias)
                  But Arachne
    Was a prodigy. All Lydia marvelled at her.

(Nymph)
    The nymphs came down from the vines on Tmolus
    As butterflies to a garden, to flock stunned
    Around what flowered out of the warp and weft
    Under her fingers.

(Minerva)
    A grace like Minerva's, unearthly,
    Moves her hands whether she bundles the fleeces
    Or teases out the wool, like cirrus,
    Or spins the yarn, and finally
    Conjures her images into their places.

(Lydian)
Surely, only Minerva could have taught her!

(Arachne) [*laughing*]
My sole instructor is my inborn skill.

Arachne
Listen: I challenge Minerva

To weave better than I weave,
And if she wins, let her do whatever she wants with me,
I shan't care.

(Minerva)
Minerva came to Arachne

As an old woman:

(Old) Minerva [*panting, leaning on stick*]
Some things that age brings
Are to be welcomed. Old experience teaches
The thread of consequence cannot be broken.

Listen to my warning: give to mortals
The tapestries that make you
Famous and foremost among mortal weavers,
But give to the goddess
Your gratitude for the gift.

Leave it to her to boast for you, if she wants to,
And ask her to forgive you
For your reckless remarks
Against her.
She will hear and she will be merciful.

[*Arachne turns from the loom,*
rears like a cobra, scowls
and nearly strikes the old woman.]

Arachne

Your brain totters

Like your decrepit body.
You have lived too long.
If you possess daughters or granddaughters
Waste your babble on them.

I make up my own mind,
And I think as I always did.
If the goddess dare practice what she preaches
Why doesn't she take up my challenge?

Why doesn't she come for a contest?

Minerva [*flaring up to twice the height*]
She has come.

[*The Nymphs fall prostrate.*
The Lydians bow
and hide their faces in terror.]

[*Arachne brazenly*
defies the goddess, with a glare.
Angry, she flushes red,
then pales —

but sticks to her challenge.]

(Tiresias)
Too eager

45

For the greater glory now to be won,
Arachne plunged with all her giddy vanity
Into destruction.

(Minerva)
Minerva rigged up her loom.

(Minerva *and* **Arachne)**
Both rolled their upper garments down
Under their breasts to give their arms freedom

For every inspiration.

[*Both concentrate on the outcome.*]

(All)
The shuttles began to fly.

[*Music and weaving.*]

(Minerva)
Minerva portrayed the divine
History of her city, Athens,
And how it came to be named.
There were the twelve high gods surrounding Jove.

Jove in his majesty and thunders.
And herself, with a shield and a long spear.

Then the goddess
Filled each corner with an illustration
Of the kind of punishment

Arachne could now expect for her impudence:
In one corner, two snowy summits,
Rhodope and Haemon – human
Before they assumed
The names of the greatest gods.

In another corner the Queen of the Pygmies
Who had challenged Juno and lost
Had become a crane.
In the third corner Antigone,

Who had challenged Juno, cried in vain
As the goddess turned her into a stork.

In the fourth corner the Assyrian King
Embracing the temple steps – all that remain
Of his daughters – his tears
Splashing the stones.
Finally

With an embroidered border of tangled olives –
Minerva framed her design.

[*Pause.*]

(Arachne)
Arachne's tapestry followed a different theme:

[*Music and weaving.*]

Across the growing pattern, Jupiter
Varied and multiplied
His amorous transformations.

A bull glistening with sweat,
Carrying off Europa.

A storming eagle
Gripping Asteria in his talons,
Asteria fighting to keep her clothes on.

Leda, bared
Under the blizzard of a swan.

A satyr
Planting Antiope with her divine twins.

The lap of Danae opens
To a shower of gold.

Arachne captured them all as if she had copied
Each as it happened.

Here Jupiter has gone into the eye of a candle,
        [*consoling*]
There he's a shepherd,   [*giving a flute*]
There a freckled serpent.   [*overcoming*]

In each of these, Arachne
Gave Jove rich new life.

Arachne bordered her picture
With a sparkling wreath of cunningly knotted
Flowers and ivy.

[*Music and weaving concludes.*]

          So. It is finished.

(Minerva)
And neither the goddess
Nor jealousy herself
Could find a stitch in the entire work
That was not perfect.
Arachne's triumph
Was unbearable.

Minerva tore from the loom
That gallery of divine indiscretions
And ripped it to rags.

[*All her power gone
into exasperation, Minerva strikes Arachne*

*with her boxwood shuttle:
one, two, three, four blows between the eyes. Arachne
staggers away groaning with indignation.*]

(Tiresias)
Arachne refused to live

With this injustice. Making a noose
And fitting it round her neck
She jumped into air, jerked at the rope's end,
And dangled, and spun.

(Minerva)
    Pity touched Minerva.

Minerva [*catching the swinging girl*]
    You have been wicked
    Enough to dangle there for ever
    And so you shall. But alive,
    And your whole tribe the same through all time
    Populating the earth.

(Tiresias)
    The goddess
    Squeezed onto the dangling Arachne
    Venom from Hecate's deadliest leaf.

(Chorus)
    Under that styptic drop
    The poor girl's head shrank to a poppy seed

    And her hair fell out.
    Her eyes, her ears, her nostrils
    Diminished beyond being. Her body
    Became a tiny ball.
    And now she is all belly

    With a dot of head. She retains
    Only her slender skilful fingers
    For legs. And so for ever
    She hangs from the thread that she spins
    Out of her belly;

Or ceaselessly weaves it
Into patterned webs
On a loom of leaves and grasses –
Her touches
Deft and swift and light as when they were human.

[*Music and spinning.*]

PART TWO

MYRRHA

    Procul hinc natae, procul este parente
    aut, mea si vestras mulcebunt carmina mentes,
    desit in hac mihi parte fides, nec credite factum,
    vel, si credetis, facti quoque credite poenam.

(Chorus)
    The story I am now going to tell you
    Is so horrible
    That fathers with daughters, wherever you are,
    Had better not listen to it.
    I beg you to stay clear.
    Or, if you find my song irresistible,
    Let your ear
    Now become incredulous.
    May you convince yourselves this never happened.

    Or, if you find yourselves
    Believing this crime and horrified by it,
    You must, above all, believe
    In the punishment, the awesome punishment
    The gods allotted to it.

    Hatred for one's father is a crime.
    Myrrha's love for her father
    Was a crime infinitely worse.

    Cinyras, the son of Pephos,
    Might well have been known as 'Fortune's Darling'
    If only he'd stayed childless.

(Cinyras)
> The court of King Cinyras hummed with suitors.
> From every degree of the compass they had come,
> The princes of the East –
> Haughty rivals for the King's daughter
> Who wanted nothing to do with any of them.

(Chorus)
> Choose, Myrrha, before the story twists,
> Choose from all these men in your father's palace –
> Excluding only one.

> Whatever arrow pierced the heart of Myrrha
> Cupid absolutely disowns it.
> Myrrha felt the stirring secret serpent of her craving
> And the horror that came with it.

Myrrha
> What is happening to me?
> What am I planning?
> You watchers in heaven,
> Help me to strangle this.
> I pray
> By the sacred bond between child and parent,
> Let me be spared this.
> Do not permit this criminal desire
> To carry me off – if it is criminal.
> Is it criminal?
> Is it unnatural?
> For all the creatures it is natural –
> When the bull mounts the heifer, his daughter,
> Neither feels shame.
> A stallion fights to breed from his own daughter.
> A billy goat will impregnate his daughter
> As soon as any other little nanny.
> And the birds – the birds –

No delicate distinctions deter them.
All mate where they can.
How lucky they are, those innocents,
Living within such liberties.
Man has distorted that licence –
Man has made new laws from his jealousy
To deprive nature of its nature.
I was born into the prison of this palace,
A prisoner of these laws.
And yet, by every contract and custom,
Cinyras owns my love.
It would be a crime indeed to withold it.
And if it were not for one small accident –
That he begat me –
I could give him my love, as his bride.

But – because I am his – he can never be mine.
How if I were a stranger?
I should get away,
Get out of this land – but could I ever
Get out of my guilt? Out of my love?
My evil obsession keeps me here
Where I can be near him,
Look at him, speak to him, touch him, kiss him,
Though that is the limit of it.
Wretch, what more can you hope for?
Do you want to lie netted
In a mesh of family conundrums –
Sister to your son,
Co-wife to your mother, your brother's mother?
Remember the Furies,
The snake-haired, dreadful sisters
Who climb from the hell of conscience
Whirling their torches.
Be careful. While you are still guiltless,

Before you have set a foot wrong,
Do not so much as think of taking
The first step. Mighty Nature
Set this prohibition
Between a human father and his daughter.
Fear it.

(Cinyras)
Meanwhile
Cinyras was wholly preoccupied
By the superfluity of suitors.
He saw only one solution.
He cited their names and lands and possessions
To his daughter –
Then simply asked her:
'Now, choose'.

(Chorus)
Long minutes
Myrrha stood staring at her father.

(Myrrha)
For her, nothing else existed.
Her brain stormed – but to no purpose,
While her eyes brimmed as if they melted.

(Cinyras)
Cinyras pitied his child.
What he saw was modesty tormented.

[*He dries her face and kisses her.*]

'Don't cry.
Just tell me,
What kind of a husband would you like?'

Myrrha [whispers]
One like you.

Cinyras [*not understanding what we know, laughing*]
My darling, never let anything change your devotion
To me!

[*Myrrha stands there
like a beast at the altar, head hanging.*]

(Singer)
Noctis erat medium, curasque et corpora somnus
solverat.

(Chorus)
Midnight. Mankind sprawled
In sleep without a care.
But Myrrha writhes in her sheets.

(Myrrha)
To cool the fiery gnawings throughout her body
She draws deep gasping breaths.
Half of her prays wildly –
In despair under the crushing
Impossibility – and half of her coolly
Plots how to put it to the test.
She was both aghast at her own passion
And reckless to satisfy it.

Like a great tree that sways,
All but cut through by the axe,
Uncertain which way to fall,
Waiting for the axe's deciding blow,
Myrrha,
Bewildered by the opposite onslaughts
Of her lust and her conscience,
Swayed, and waited to fall.
Either way, she saw only death.

Her lust, consummated, had to be death;
Denied, had to be death.

(**Chorus**)
    With a huge effort
    She got out of bed,
    Tied her girdle to a door lintel
    And made a noose.

Myrrha [*sobbing*]
    Cinyras. O my darling,
    When you see this, please understand it.

    [*She pushes her face*
    through the noose. As she draws the knot
    tight to the nape of her neck –
    she faints. The lintel jerks at her weight.]

(**Chorus**)
    Her old Nurse lay in the next room.

    [*The Nurse is instantly up and through the door.*
    She shrieks,
    tugs the knot loose,
    lays the limp Myrrha on the floor,
    thinking she is dead. The Nurse
    tears her own garments, and beats at her breasts.
    Myrrha recovers.

    The Nurse embraces her and weeps.]

(**Nurse**)
    Why should you want to do such a thing?

[*Myrrha*
lies there,
silent.

The Nurse claws at her own shrivelled breasts.]

By this ruin
Of the cradle of your first years,
Tell your old nurse your secret.

[*Myrrha twists away.*]

Nurse
    I may be old,
    But that may make it easier for me to help you.
    If some lunatic fit has fallen on you
    From some power in the air,
    From something you have eaten, some place you
        have sat in,
    I know who can cure it.
    If somebody has bewitched you, I know
    The rituals to unwind the spell and bind it
    Round the witch's neck.
    Or if you have unsettled the gods
    I know which offerings can appease them.
    What else can it be?
    Your home and future are secure;
    Your father and mother are happy, they reign in
        their prime.

[*The single word 'father' goes through Myrrha*
like a hot iron, and she sighs in misery.
The Nurse, missing the clue, nevertheless perceives
love explains Myrrha's behaviour.
The Nurse tightly embraces Myrrha.]

61

Nurse
I know, I know your sickness.
You are in love.
And I am the very one who can best help you.
Not a breath of this shall come to your father.

Myrrha [*choking at the word 'father'*]
Go away.

[*she wrenches herself
from the Nurse's clasp
and buries her head in her pillows*]

[*sobbing*] Leave me alone.

[*the Nurse persists*]

Stop. Don't ask.
What you are wanting to know is pure evil.

[*The Nurse recoils.
She trembles with fear.*

Yet she's determined to pursue the truth.]

(Nurse) [*clasping Myrrha's feet*]
I'll tell your father everything
About that noose
Unless you share your secret –
I promise you my perfect discretion
If you will confide it.
Yes, and I'll help. I promise you my help.

[*Myrrha looks up and flings her arms
around the Nurse.
Myrrha tries to confess –*

and –
eventually –]

Myrrha

My mother is so lucky
To have such a man for her husband –

[*Myrrha is overwhelmed
by sobs.*]

(Nurse)

The nurse had heard enough.
Now she knew she had the truth
And she felt her body go cold.

[*Myrrha notices the Nurse's coldness.*]

(Myrrha)

If I cannot satisfy myself,
No matter what I destroy in the act,
Then I am happy to die right now.

Nurse

This is great folly.
Death is never an option, only an error.
Myrrha, you shall have –

[*pause – she can't bring herself to say 'your father'*]

You shall have – I promise it, I call
Heaven to witness – you shall have your will.

(Chorus)

Now came the festival of Ceres.

(Singer)

Prima Ceres unco glaebam dimovit aratro,
prima dedit fruges alimentaque mitia terris,
prima dedit leges; Cereris sunt omnia munus;
illa canenda mihi est. utinam modo dicere possim
carmina digna dea! certe dea carmine digna est.

[*Hughes' translation:*
Ceres was the first
To split open the grassland with a ploughshare.
The first
To plant corn and nurse harvests.
She was the first to give man laws.

Everything man has he owes to Ceres.
So now I sing of her
And so I pray my song may be worthy
Of this great goddess,
For surely she is worthy of the song.]

(Chorus)

Married women, robed in laundered whiteness,
Bring the goddess the first-fruits
Of the harvest. For these women,
Through nine days and nights,
Love, or the slightest contact with a man,
Is forbidden.

Cenchreis, the wife of Cinyras,
The mother Myrrha so painfully envied,
Was one of the celebrants
Wrapped in the white gown of the mysteries.
Nine days and nine nights
The King's bed was to be empty.

That first evening Cinyras drowsily
Sipping a last glass, found himself
Listening to the nurse's strange news –

(Nurse)
An incredibly beautiful girl;
She's madly in love with you.

(Cinyras)
How old?

Nurse
Same as Myrrha.

Cinyras
Bring her tonight.

Nurse [*returning to Myrrha*]
Success, success.

[*Myrrha shivers
with the quick touch of a shadow of terror.
Then she lets her joy lift her off her feet.*]

(Chorus)
The moon had gone down,
Clouds covered the stars,
When Myrrha, like a wide-eyed sleepwalker,
Hypnotised by a dream of wild lust,
Stepped from her chamber –
The heavens above gave her no light.

(Nurse)
Three times
Myrrha stumbled.
Three times
A screech owl
Salutes her evil fate.

[Myrrha ignores all omens,
hiding from her shame
in the darkness.

Her left hand
clings to the hand of the Nurse.
Her right hand
gropes for invisible obstacles
as if she were blind.
The Nurse goes swiftly –
she knows the map of the palace with her eyes closed.]

(Nurse)
Here
Is the door of the King's bedroom.

(Myrrha)
Suddenly Myrrha is standing
In the dark chamber
Where the King breathes.

[Myrrha's legs almost go from beneath her.
The blood drains from her face and head –
Unrecognised, she knows
She still has time to get out.

More and more horrified by herself,
More and more sick with guilt,
Myrrha lets her old nurse
Lead her toward the bed where the King waits.]

Nurse *[whispers to Cinyras]*
She is yours.

[*The Nurse gently pushes Myrrha forward –*
Until Myrrha's reluctant, trembling body
Lifts weightless, propelling itself
Towards the King, her father's bed.

The nurse crabs away into the darkness,
fleeing the inevitable.]

(Chorus)
The father
Welcomed his own flesh and blood
Into the luxury of the royal bed.
He comforted her,
Mistaking her whimpering struggle of lust and
    conscience
For girlish panic.
It could be
To soothe her he called her

Cinyras

My child

(Chorus)
Or even

Cinyras
My daughter

(Chorus)
And maybe when she called him

Myrrha

Father

(Chorus)
He supposed that made her first yielding
Somehow easier for her –
So the real crime, that the King thought no crime,
Let nothing of its wickedness be omitted.

67

After her father had crammed her with his seed
Myrrha left him
Finding her way now without difficulty –
Her womb satisfied
With its prize:
A child conceived in evil.

The next night father and daughter did it again
In the pitch darkness.
The same, night after night. On the ninth night
Cinyras made a mistake.
He let curiosity take over.

[*Cinyras lights a lamp,
holds it aloft
revealing his daughter.*

*A roar throughout the palace.
He snatches his sword from its scabbard.
Myrrha dives from his chamber
escaping into the night.*]

(Myrrha)
Myrrha crossed her father's kingdom,
Left Arabia's palms far behind her.
Till a nine-month meandering journey
Brought her to Sabea.
There she rested the kicking freight
That she could carry no further,
Utterly disgusted with her life
But afraid of dying.
She had no idea what to pray for,
So prayed without thinking:

Myrrha
    O you gods,
    If there are any gods with patience enough
    To listen to me
    Who deserve
    The most pitiless judgement
    Which I would welcome –
    Remove me
    From life and from death
    Into some nerveless limbo.

(Chorus)
    A power in the air hears the last prayer
    Of the desperate.

    The earth gripped both her ankles as she prayed.
    Roots force from beneath her toenails, they burrow
    Among deep stones to the bedrock. She sways:

    In that moment, her bones become grained wood,
    Their marrow pith,

    Her blood sap, her arms boughs, her fingers twigs,
    Her skin rough bark. And already
    The gnarling crust has coffined her swollen womb.

    It swarms over her breasts. It warps upwards
    Reaching for her eyes as she bows
    Eagerly into it, hurrying the burial

Of her face and her hair under thick-webbed bark.
Now all her feeling has gone into wood, with her body.
Yet she weeps,

The warm drops ooze from her rind.
These tears are still treasured.
To this day they are known by her name: Myrrh.
Meanwhile the meaty fruit her father implanted
Has ripened in the bole. Past its term,
It heaves to rive a way out of its mother.

But Myrrha's cramps are clamped in the heart-wood's
    vice.
Her gagged convulsions cannot leak a murmur.

Yet a mother's agony
Strained in the creaking tree and her tears drench it.
For pity, heaven's midwife

Lays her hands on the boughs in their torment
As she recites the necessary magic.
The trunk erupts, the bark splits, and there tumbles

Out into the world with a shattering yell
The baby Adonis.

(Bacchus–Silenus)
Peasants crowded to gawp at Silenus –
The end-product of a life
They could not imagine.
They chained him with flowers and dragged him,
To their king.

(Midas)
Midas recognised him,
And honoured him, fat and old and drunk as he was,
As the companion of Bacchus,
And restored him to the god,

(Bacchus)
Bacchus was so grateful –

'Any wish,
Whatever you want,
It will be granted'.

(Midas)
He did not have to rack his brains.
A certain fantasy
Hovered in his head perpetually,
Wistfully fondled all his thoughts by day,
Manipulated all his dreams by night.
Now it saw its chance and seized his tongue.

Midas
Here is my wish:
Let whatever I touch become gold.
Yes, gold, the finest, the purest, the brightest.

71

(Bacchus) [*sighs*]
    Bacchus felt pity –
    Yet his curiosity was intrigued
    To see how such stupidity would be punished.
    So he granted the wish, then stood back to watch.

    The Phrygian King returned through the garden
    Eager to test the power –

(Midas)
                         yet apprehensive
    That he had merely dreamed and now was awake,
    Where alchemy never works.

(Bacchus)
                        He broke a twig
    From a low branch of oak.

(Midas)
                    The leaves
    Turned to heavy gold as he stared at them
    And his mouth went dry.

(Bacchus)
    He picked up a stone and weighed it in his hand

(Midas)
    As it doubled its weight, then doubled again,
    And became bright yellow.

(Bacchus)
    He brushed his hand over a clump of grass,

(Midas)
    The blades stayed bent – soft ribbons
    Of gold foil. A ripe ear of corn
    Was crisp and dry and light as he plucked it

But a heavy slug of gold, intricately braided,
As he rolled it between his palms.

(Bacchus)
It was then that a cold thought seemed to whisper.

(Midas)
He had wanted to chew the milky grains –
But none broke chaffily free from their pockets.
The ear was gold – its grain inedible,
Inaccessibly solid with the core.

[*Midas frowns.*]

(Bacchus)
He reached for a hanging apple.

(Midas)
With a slight twist he took the sudden weight.

(Bacchus)
He made no attempt to bite, as he pondered its colour.

He washed his hands under flowing water, at a
    fountain.

(Midas)
Already a hope
Told him that the gift might wash away,
As waking up will wash out a nightmare.

(Bacchus)
But the water that touched him
Coiled into the pool below as plumes
Of golden smoke, settling heavily
In a silt of gold atoms.

[Suddenly he sweats.
He sits
at the table
and reaches for a roasted bird: the carcase
topples from his horrified fingers
into his dish with a clunk.
He reaches for bread: he cannot break it:
it is gold.
In terror,
he reaches for the goblet of wine.
Taking his time, he pours in water,
swirls the mix,
sets his lips to the cold rim:
wet gold shines on his lips
as he lowers the cup.
Others, already dumbfounded
by what they have seen, are now aghast.
Midas spits gold mush.
He gets up from his chair, reeling,
as if poisoned.]

(Bacchus)
He fell on his bed, face down.

[The bedclothes turn to gold.]

Midas *[prays]*

                      I have been a fool.
Forgive me, Bacchus. Forgive the greed
That made me so stupid.
Forgive me for a dream
That had not touched the world
Where gold is truly gold and nothing but.
Save me from my own shallowness,
Where I shall drown in gold
And be buried in gold.

Nothing can live, I see, in a world of gold.

[*Pause.*]

Bacchus [*kindly*]
I return you
To your happier human limitations.
But now you must wash away
The last stain of the curse
You begged for and preferred to every blessing.
A river goes by Sardis. Follow it upstream.
Find the source
Which gushes from a cliff and plunges
Into a rocky pool. Plunge with it.
Go completely under. Let that river
Carry your folly away and leave you clean.

(Bacchus)
Midas obeyed and the river's innocent water
Took whatever was left of the granted wish.
Even today the soil of its flood plain
Can be combed into a sparse glitter.
And big popcorns of gold, in its gravels,
Fever the fossicker.

(Midas)
Midas never got over the shock.
The sight of gold was like the thought of a bee
To one just badly stung –
It made his hair prickle, his nerves tingle.
He retired to the mountain woods
And a life of deliberate poverty. There
He worshipped Pan, who lives in the mountain caves.

75

[Pan pipes music – enter Pan.]

(Bacchus)
> King Midas was chastened
> But not really changed. He was no wiser.
> His stupidity
> Was merely lying low. Waiting, as usual,
> For another chance to ruin his life.

---

*[The Pan pipes music swells – Pan and Midas dance
and sing with the Nymphs – Bacchus leaves.]*

(Pan/Midas/Nymphs) *[singing]*

         'Redeuntem colle Lycaeo
> Pan videt hanc pinuque caput praecinctus acuta
> talia verba refert' –
> precibus spretis fugisse per avia nympham,
> donec harenosi placidum Ladonis ad amnem
> venerit;
> ut se mutarent liquidas orasse sorores,
> Panaque cum prensam sibi iam Syringa putaret,
> corpore pro nymphae calamos tenuisse palustres,
> dumque ibi suspirat, motos in harundine ventos
> effecisse sonum tenuem similemque querenti.
> arte nova vocisque deum dulcedine captum

Pan
> 'hoc mihi colloquium tecum'

(Midas/Nymphs) *[singing]*

        dixisse

Pan

          'manebit,'

(Midas/Nymphs) *[singing]*
> atque ita disparibus calamis conpagine cerae
> inter se iunctis nomen tenuisse puellae.

[*Translation from towards the end of Book I,*
Loeb edition:

'One day Pan saw Syrinx as she was coming back
from Mount Lycaeus, his head wreathed with a
crown of sharp pine-needles, and thus addressed
her' –
    the nymph, spurning his prayers, fled
through the pathless wastes until she came to Ladon's
stream flowing peacefully along his sandy banks;
    she besought her sisters of the stream to change
her form; and how Pan, when now he thought he
had caught Syrinx, instead of her held naught but
marsh reeds in his arms; and while he sighed in
disappointment, the soft air stirring in the reeds
gave forth a low complaining sound. Touched
by this wonder and charmed by the sweet tones, the
god exclaimed: 'This converse, at least, shall I have
with thee.' And so the pipes, made of unequal
reeds fitted together by a joining of wax, took and
kept the name of the maiden.]

(Juno)
Among those demi-gods, those perfect girls
Who sport about the bright source and live in it,
The beauty of Salmacis, the water-nymph,
Was perfect.

(Jupiter)
She was bending to gather lilies for a garland
When she spied Hermaphroditus.

(Juno)
At that first glimpse she knew she had to have him.

(Jupiter)
She trod on prickles until she could touch him.

(Juno)
She held back only a moment,
Checked her girdle, the swing of her hem, her
   cleavage,

(Jupiter)
Let her lust flood hot and startled
Into her cheek, eyes, lips – made her whole face
Open as a flower that offers itself,
Wet with nectar. Then she spoke:

Salmacis [*to Hermaphroditus*]
Do you mind if I say – you are beautiful?
Seen from where I stand, you could be a god.
Are you a god? If you are human,
What a lucky sister! As for the mother
Who held you, and pushed her nipple between
   your lips,
I am already sick with envy of her.
I dare not think of a naked wife in your bed.

If she exists, I dare not think of her bliss.
Let me beg a taste, one little sip
Of her huge happiness. A secret between us.
But if you are unmarried – here I am.
Let us lie down and make our own
Bridal bed, where we can love each other
To sleep. And awaken each other.

(Juno)
The boy blushed – he had no idea
What she was talking about.

(Jupiter)
Her heart lurched again when she saw
How his blush bewildered his beauty.

(Salmacis) [*sliding her arms around Hermaphroditus' neck*]
                              Give me a kiss,
One kiss, one brotherly kiss –

Hermaphroditus
Get away. Let me go,
Or I'm off.

Salmacis
            Forgive me! Forgive me!
I couldn't help it. I'm going. Oh, I'm spoiling
This lovely place for you. I'm going. I'm going.

(Juno)
She ducks behind a bush.
Her eye fixed, like the eye of a leopard.

(Jupiter)
Thinking he's utterly alone
Hermaphroditus paddles into the pool's edge,
    goes deeper.

The cool pulse of the spring, warping the clarity,
Massages his knees –

(**Hermaphroditus**) *and* (**Salmacis**)
                         – delicious.

(**Juno**)
He peels off his tunic and the air
Makes free with all that had been hidden,
Freshens his nudity.

[*Salmacis groans softly. She watches him
slap his pale shoulders, hugging himself,
and slap his belly to prepare it
for the plunge.*]

(**Jupiter**)
Suddenly he's swimming, a head bobbing.

Salmacis
I've won! He's mine!
He's mine!

(**Juno**)
                    With a couple of bounds
She hits the pool stark naked.

(**Jupiter**)
Then out of the upheaval
Her arms reach and wind round him,
And slippery as the roots of big lilies
But far stronger, her legs below wind round him.
He flounders and goes under –
Burning for air, he can do nothing –

(**Juno**)
Her hands hunt over him, her body
Knots itself
Every way around him

Like a sinewy otter
Hunting some kind of fish
That flees hither and thither inside him;
She flings and locks her coils
Around him like a snake,
And like ivy which first binds the branches
In its meshes, then pulls the whole tree down,
And as the octopus –
A tangle of constrictors, nippled with suckers –
Embraces its prey.

(Jupiter)
But still Hermaphroditus kicks to be free.

(Juno)
So she crushes her breasts and face against him
And clings to him with every inch of her surface.

Salmacis
It's no use struggling.
You can strain, wrestle, squirm, but cannot
Ever get away from me now.
The gods are listening to me.
The gods have agreed we never, never
Shall be separated, you and me.

(Juno *and* Jupiter)
The gods heard her frenzy – and smiled.

[*Juno and Jupiter smile to each other.*]

(Jupiter)
And there in the giddy boil the two bodies
Melted into a single body,
Seamless as the water.

Story-Teller
> Pandion, the King of Athens, saw
> King Tereus was as rich
> And powerful as himself.

(Pandion)
> So Pandion gave his daughter Procne to Tereus,
> And thought himself happy.

(Story-Teller)
> But Hymen and Juno and the Graces,
> Those deities who bless brides, they shunned this
> marriage.
> Instead the bridal bed was prepared by the Furies
> Who lit the married pair to it with torches
> Stolen from a funeral procession.
> Then an owl

> Flew up from its dark hole to sit on the roof
> Directly above their bed. All that night
> It interrupted their joy –
> Alternating little mewing cries
> With prophetic screams of catastrophe.
> This was the accompaniment of omens

> When Tereus, the great King of Thrace,
> Married Procne, and begot Itys.
> But all Thrace rejoiced.
> So ignorant are men.

Five years passed.

Procne [*stroking his face*]
                    If you love me
Give me the perfect gift: a sight of my sister.
Let me visit her. Or, better still,
Let her visit us. Go – promise my father
Her stay here can be just as brief as he pleases.

(Tereus)
   At a command from Tereus, oar and sail
   Brought him to Athens.

(Pandion)
                    There King Pandion
   Greeted his son-in-law.

(Tereus)
                    Tereus
   Began to explain his unexpected arrival –
   'Procne longs for just one glimpse of her sister' –
   But just as he was promising

The immediate return of Philomela –
There, mid-sentence,
She entered, arrayed
In the wealth of a kingdom,
Still unaware that her own beauty
Was the most astounding of her jewels.

Tereus felt his blood alter thickly.
He stared. Lust bristled up his thighs
And poured into the roots of his teeth.

Story-Teller
    His first thought was:

(Tereus)
                        Buy her attendants
    And her nurses with bribes.
    Then turn the girl's own head
    With priceless gifts –
    Cash in your whole kingdom for her.

Story-Teller
    His next thought was . . .

(Tereus)
    Simply to grab her
    And carry her off –
    Then fight to keep her.
    All of a sudden, wildly impatient

    He pressed Pandion again with Procne's request –
    Passion made him persuasive.
    [*weeping*] 'Procne sickens to see her sister.'

Story-Teller
    God in heaven, how blind men are!

(Philomela) [*overwhelmed; weeping, hugging Pandion*]
    As you love me and live for my happiness
    I beg you to grant me this chance –

(Tereus)
    Tereus watched her kiss and caress her father.

84

(Pandion)
    King Pandion surrendered at last
    To the doubled passion of his daughters.

(Philomela)
    Ecstatic, Philomela
    Wept and thanked him for his permission

Story-Teller
    The sun went down.
    A royal banquet glittered and steamed.
    The guests, replete, slept.

(Tereus)
    Only the Thracian King tossed,
    Remembering Philomela's every gesture,
    Remembering her lips,
    Her voice, her hair, her hands, her glances,
    And seeming to see
    Every part her garments concealed
    Just as he wanted it.
    So he fed his lust and stared at the darkness.

Story-Teller
    Dawn lit the wharf at last

    For their departure.

Pandion
    By your honour, by the gods, by the bond between us,
    Protect her like a father.

    Send her home soon,
    This darling of my old age.

    [*Pandion embraces Philomela and weeps.*]

(Pandion)
Give me your hands, as seals of your promise,
Carry my blessing
To my far-off daughter and grandson, Itys.

Story-Teller
There the father choked
On his goodbye.
Overwhelmed of a sudden
By fear –

(Pandion)
Inexplicable, icy,
A gooseflesh of foreboding.

(Philomela)
The oars bent and the wake broadened
Behind the painted ship.
Philomela watched the land sinking.

Tereus [*laughing softly*]
I've won. My prayers are granted. She is mine.

(Philomela)
The moment the ship touched his own shore
Tereus lifted Philomela
Onto a horse, and hurried her
To a fort, behind high walls,
Hidden in deep forest.
And there he imprisoned her.

Bewildered and defenceless,
Failing to understand anything
And in a growing fear of everything,
She begged him to bring her to her sister.
His answer was to rape her – ignoring her screams
To her father, to her sister, to the gods.

(Tereus)
Afterwards, she crouched in a heap, shuddering –
Like a lamb still clinging to life
After the wolf has savaged it
And for some reason dropped it.
Or like a dove, a bloody rag, still alive
Under the talons that stand on it.

[*Like a woman in mourning*
Philomela gouges her arms with her nails,
Claws her hair, and pounds her breasts with her fists.]

Philomela

                                    You disgusting savage!
You sadistic monster!
The oaths my father bound you to –
Were they meaningless?
Do you remember his tears – you are inhuman,
You couldn't understand them.
What about my sister waiting for me?
What about me?
What about my life?
What about your marriage?
You have dragged us all
Into your bestial pit!
How can my sister think of me now?
Your crime is only half done –
Kill me and complete it.
But the gods are watching –
If they bother to notice what has happened –
If they are more than the puffs of air
That go with their names –

Then you will answer for this.
I may be lost,
But I have my voice.
And shame will not stop me.
I shall tell everything
To your own people, yes, to all Thrace.
Even if you keep me here
Every leaf in this forest
Will become a tongue to tell my story.
The dumb rocks will witness.
All heaven will be my jury.
Every god in heaven will judge you.

[*Speechless,
in a confusion of fear and fury,*

*Tereus hauls Philomela up by the hair,
twists her arms behind her back and binds them.
Then he draws his sword.
Eagerly, Philomela bends her head backwards,
closes her eyes, offers her throat to the blade.*

*Still calling to her father
And to the gods
And still trying to curse him,
Tereus catches her tongue with bronze pincers,
drags it out to its full length
and slices it off at the root.*]

Story-Teller
The tongue squirmed in the dust, babbling on –
Shaping words that were now soundless.

88

After this, again and again –
Though I can hardly bear to think about it,
Let alone believe it – the obsessed King
Like an automaton
Returned to the body he had mutilated
For his gruesome pleasure.

(Tereus)
Then, stuffing the whole hideous business
Deep among his secrets,
He came home, smooth-faced, to his wife.

(Procne)
Where is my sister?

(Tereus)
                    She is dead.

Story-Teller
His grief, as he wept, convinced everybody.

(Procne)
Procne stripped off her royal garments
And wrapped herself in black. She built a tomb
Without a body for her sister,

Story-Teller
And there she made offerings to a ghost
That did not exist, mourning the fate of a sister
Who endured a fate utterly different.

A year went by. Philomela,
Staring at the massive stone walls
And stared at by the guards, was still helpless,
Locked up in her dumbness and her prison.
But frustration, prolonged, begets invention,
And a vengeful anger nurses it.

(Woman Servant)
>   She set up a Thracian loom
>   And wove on a white fabric scarlet symbols
>   That told in detail what had happened to her.
>   A servant, who understood her gestures
>   But knew nothing of what she carried,
>   Took this gift to Procne, the Queen.

(Procne) [*unrolling the tapestry*]
>   Procne saw
>   The only interpretation
>   Was the ruin of her life.

>   [*Procne sits there, silent and unmoving,
>   As if thinking of something else entirely.*]

(Procne)
>   In those moments, her restraint
>   Was superhuman. But grief so sudden, so huge,
>   Made mere words seem paltry.
>   None could lift to her lips
>   One drop of bitterness.
>   And tears were pushed aside

>   By the devouring single idea
>   Of revenge. Revenge
>   Had swallowed her whole being. She had plunged
>   Into a labyrinth of plotting
>   Where good and evil, right and wrong,
>   Forgot their differences.

>   [*Cymbals and song – the festival of Bacchus.*]

(Singer)
>   Tempus erat, quo sacra solent trieterica Bacchi

90

Sithoniae celebrare nurus: (nox conscia sacris,
nocte sonat Rhodope tinnitibus aeris acuti)
nocte sua est egressa domo regina deique
ritibus instruitur furialiaque accipit arma

Story-Teller
Now came the festival of Bacchus
Celebrated every third year
By the young women of Thrace.

(Procne)
Dressed as a worshipper
Procne joined the uproar.

[*Procne carries a light spear,*
vine leaves round her head, and a deer pelt
slung over her left shoulder –
a Bacchante.]

Story-Teller

                                    Beserk
She hurled herself through the darkness, terrifying.

(Procne)
She found the hidden fort in the forest.
Procne freed her sister,

[*Procne disguises Philomela as a Bacchante.*]

And brought her home to the palace.

Story-Teller
Philomela felt she might die
Of sheer fear, when she realised
She was in the house of her ravisher.

*[In shame, Philomela does not look at her sister, Procne:
Philomela fixes her eyes on the ground like a
    madwoman.]*

Procne

Tears can't help us,
Only the sword;
Or if it exists,
Something more pitiless
Even than the sword.

O my sister, nothing now
Can soften
The death Tereus is going to die.
Let me see this palace one flame
And Tereus a blazing insect in it,
Making it brighter.

Let me break his jaw. Hang him up
By his tongue and saw it through with a broken knife.
Then dig his eyes from their holes.
Give me the strength, you gods,
To twist his hips and shoulders from their sockets
And butcher the limbs off his trunk

Till his soul for very terror scatter
Away through a thousand exits.
Let me kill him – Oh! However we kill him
Our revenge has to be something
That will appal heaven and hell
And stupefy the earth.

[*Enter Itys.*]

(Itys)

While Procne raved Itys came in –
'Mummy, mummy!'

(Procne)

. . .

Her heart ice,
She saw what had to be done.

[*Itys runs to her,*
his five-year-old arms
pulling to her, to be kissed
and to kiss her. He chatters lovingly
through his loving laughter.
Procne's heart shrinks.]

Her fury seemed to be holding its breath
For that moment
As tears burned her eyes. She felt
Her love for this child
Softening her ferocious will.

[*Procne looks back at Itys –*
and then at her sister, crying.]

Procne

He tells me all his love – but she
Has no tongue to utter a word of hers.
He can call me mother, but she
Cannot call me sister.

This is the man you have married!
Oh daughter of Pandion!

93

You are your father's shame and his despair.
To love this monster Tereus, or pity him,
You must be a monster.
It is monstrous!

[*Procne catches Itys by the arm
and drags him to a far cellar of the palace.
Itys sees what's coming
and tries to clasp her neck.*]

Itys
Mama, Mama!

Story-Teller
Staring into his face
Procne pushed a sword through his chest –
Then
Slashed his throat.

Now the two sisters
Ripped the hot little body
Into pulsating gobbets.
The room was awash with blood
As they cooked his remains – some of it
Gasping in bronze pots, some weeping on spits.

(Procne)
A feast followed. Procne invited
One guest only, her husband.

[*Tereus lolls,
ignorant, happy,
swallows, smiles.*]

Tereus
Where is Itys? Bring him!

Procne

    Your son is here, already.

    He is here, inside,

    He could not be closer to you.

Tereus (*suspecting some joke, he looks beneath the throne*)

    Itys! Come out,

    Show yourself!

    [*The doors bang wide open.*

    Philomela bursts into the throne-room,

    her hair and gown bloody. She rushes forward,

    and her hands, red to the elbows,

    jam into the face of Tereus

    a crimson, dripping ball:

    the head of Itys.

    Some moments. Tereus' brain

    refuses to make sense of it.

    The joy she cannot speak, Philomela releases in

      a scream.

    Then:

    Tereus roars from every fibre in his body.

    He heaves the table aside.]

(Tereus)

    Furies,

    Come up out of hell!

    [*Tereus staggers,*

    tugs at his rib-cage

    as if he might

    empty out what he has eaten.

He sobs.]

I am the tomb of my boy.

[*Tereus grips his sword-hilt and steadies himself*

As he sees his sisters running.
He bellows
an anguished
homicidal bellow.]

Story-Teller
    He came after them and they
    Who had been running seemed to be flying.

    And suddenly they were flying. One swerved
    On wings into the forest,
    The other, with the blood still on her breast,
    Flew up under the eaves of the palace.
    And Tereus, charging blind
    In his delirium of grief and vengeance,

    No longer caring what happened –
    He too was suddenly flying.
    On his head and shoulders a crest of feathers,
    Instead of a sword a long curved beak –
    Like a warrior transfigured
    With battle-frenzy dashing into battle.

(Tereus)
    He had become a hoopoe.

(Philomela)
Philomela mourned in the forest,
A nightingale.

(Procne)
Procne lamented round and round the palace,
A swallow.

[*Birdsong.*]

(Bacchus)
The cliff-face of Tmolus watches
Half the Mediterranean. It falls away
To Sardis on one side, and on the other
To the village of Hypaepa.
Pan lives in a high cave on that cliff.
He was amusing himself,
Showing off to the nymphs
Thrilling them out of their airy bodies
With the wild airs
He breathed through the reeds of his flute.

[*Music.*]

Their ecstasies flattered him,
But the flattered
Become fools.

(Pan) [*assuring the nymphs*]
Apollo, no less,
Steals my tunes and rearranges my rhythms –

(Bacchus)
So it was a shock
For Pan
To find himself staring at the great god Apollo
Half eclipsed with black rage,
Half beaming with a friendly challenge.

Apollo
Tmolus, the mountain, can judge us.

(Bacchus)
Tmolus shook out his hair,
Freed his ears of bushes, trees, birds, insects,

Then took his place at the seat of judgement.

Tmolus
 [*to Pan*] Your music first.

 [*Pan's music – the Nymphs are ecstatic.*]

(Bacchus)
 Tmolus smiled,
 As if coming awake –

(Tmolus)
 Back, he thought, hugely refreshed
 From a journey through himself.

(Bacchus)
 But now he turned
 To Apollo, the great, bright sun-god.

(Apollo)
 Apollo was serious.
 In his left hand the lyre
 Was a model, in magical code,
 Of the earth and heavens.
 In his right hand he held
 The plectrum that could touch
 Every wavelength in the Universe
 Singly or simultaneously.
 Even his posture
 Was like a tone – like a tuning fork,
 Vibrant, alerting the whole earth,
 Bringing heaven down to listen.

 [*Apollo's even brighter music.*

Tmolus and the Nymphs decompose
helplessly dissolving
among the harmonics.]

(Pan) [*humbled*]

                              Yes,
   Apollo is the master.

   [*The Nymphs gaze at Apollo. They agree.*]

Midas
   The judgement
   Is ignorant, stupid, and merely favours power.
   Apollo's efforts
   Are nothing but interior decoration
   By artificial light, for the chic, the effete.
   Pan is the real thing – the true voice
   Of the subatomic.

(Bacchus)
   Apollo's face seemed to writhe
   Momentarily
   As he converted this clown's darkness to light,

(Apollo)
   Then he pointed his plectrum at the ears
   That had misheard so grievously.

(Bacchus)
   Abruptly those ears lolled long and animal,
   On either side of King Midas' impertinent face –
   Grey-whiskered, bristly,
   The familiar ears of a big ass.

(Midas) [*grabs his new ears*]
   Then he had some seconds of pure terror

Waiting for the rest of his body to follow.

(Apollo)
    But this was the god's decision: Midas
    Lived on, human, wagging the ears of a donkey.

(Midas)
    Midas crept away.
    Every few paces he felt at his ears and groaned.
    He slunk back to his palace. He needed
    Comfort. He was bitterly disillusioned
    With the spirit of the wilderness.
    He hid those ears – in a turban superb
    As compensation could be.

(Barber)
    But a king needs a barber.
    Sworn to secrecy or impalement,
    The barber, wetting his lips,
    Clipped around the gristly roots
    Of the great angling ears as if the hair there
    Might be live nerve-ends.
    What he was staring at,
    And having to believe, was worse
    For him than for their owner,
    Almost. He had to hide this news
    As if it were red-hot
    Under his tongue, and keep it there.
    The ultimate shame-secret
    Of the ruler of the land.
    It struggled to blurt
    Itself out, whenever
    He opened his mouth.
    It made him sweat and often

Gasp aloud, or strangle
A groan to a sigh. Or wake up
In the middle of the silent night
Certain he had just
Yelled it out, at the top of his voice,
To the whole city.
He knew
He had to spit it out somehow.

In the lawn of a park he lifted a turf
After midnight. He kneeled there
And whispered into the raw hole:

Barber
  Ass's ears! Midas has ass's ears!

(Barber)
  Then he fitted the turf back, trod flat the grave
  Of that insuppressible gossip,
  And went off, singing
  Under his breath.

(Reeds)
  But in no time,
  A clump of reeds bunched out.
  It looked strange, on the park lawn,
  But sounded stranger.
  Every gust brought an inarticulate whisper
  Out of the bending stalks. At every puff
  They betrayed the barber's confidence,
  Broadcasting the buried secret:

Reeds [*hissing*]
  Ass's ears! Ass's ears! Midas has ass's ears!
  Ass's ears! Midas has ass's ears!

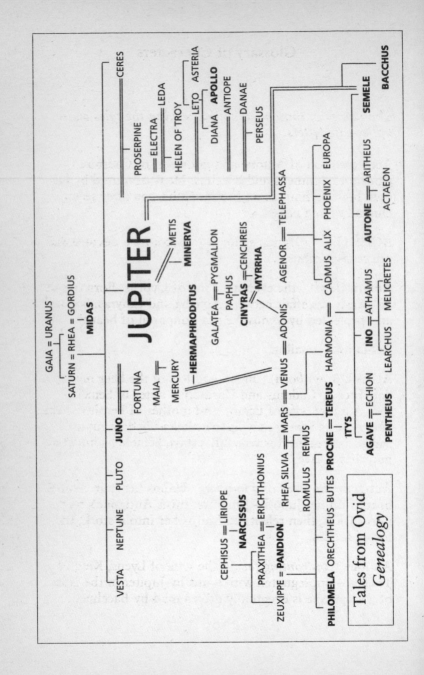

Tales from Ovid
Genealogy

Glossary of Characters

The names of those who are featured in the tales are in upper-case letters.

Actaeon son of Autone and grandson of Cadmus. Cousin of Pentheus and Bacchus. He is devoured by his own hunting hounds on Mount Cithaeron after seeing Diana bathing naked.

ACOETES a Lydian sailor who becomes a devotee and priest of Bacchus.

Adonis (*lord*) the eventual King of Cyprus. Born out of an incestuous affair between Myrrha and Cinyras. Beloved and protected by Venus, he is a nonpareil of beauty.

Aethalion a sailor.

AGAVE (*high-born*) moon goddess of the beer revels, a daughter of Cadmus and Harmonia, sister of Semele, Ino, Autone, wife of Echion and mother of Pentheus. She bad-mouths Semele, saying Semele had lied about how she got pregnant, for which Bacchus, Semele's son, later punishes Agave.

Antigone (*in place of a mother*) claims her hair is more beautiful than Juno's – Juno first turns Antigone's hair into snakes, then relents and turns her into a stork, the foe of snakes.

Antiope (*confronting face*) the wife of Lycus, King of Thebes – impregnated with twins by Jupiter in the guise of a satyr. She is eventually driven mad by Bacchus.

APOLLO (*destroyer*)   the sun god, the son of Jupiter and
Leto. Music, poetry, astronomy, mathematics, medicine
and science are within his sphere. He stands for moder-
ation in all things, yet he's also a warrior like his sister
Diana. A god of outstanding beauty and great stature.

ARACHNE (*spider*)   a daughter of a Lydian dyer in
Phocaea – famed for its purple dye – who gains a
reputation for weaving and embroidery but will not
attribute this talent to anyone but herself – certainly not
to the goddess of weavers, Minerva.

Asteria (*of the starry sky, of the sun*)   ravished by
Jupiter in the guise of an eagle, she transforms into a
quail to escape him, throws herself into the sea and
becomes the island of Ortygia (Quail Island) now called
Delos.

AUTONE (*with a mind of her own*)   daughter of
Cadmus, sister of Semele, Ino and Agave, the aunt of
Pentheus and Bacchus, the mother of Actaeon. She joins
her sisters during the Bacchante revels in attacking
Pentheus on Mount Cithaeron – where her son Acteaon
was torn limb from limb by his hunting hounds.

BACCHUS (*raging*)   son of Jupiter and Semele, twice-
born, and cousin of Pentheus. Given to King Athamas
and his wife Ino (Semele's sister) to rear so Juno would
not find him. She does, so Bacchus is entrusted to the
nymphs of Nysa with Silenus as his moral tutor. On
reaching manhood, Bacchus discovers the vine, wine and
wanderlust. Eventually he returns to Thebes where his
cousin Pentheus reigns. Bacchus introduces his revels in
which the whole populous, especially the women, are
seized with mystical ecstacy – inflamed by the narcotic
qualities of raw mushrooms (his wild Autumnal feast

was called 'The Ambrosia'). His followers would annoint their hair with myrrh, an aphrodisiac. The god of wine, ecstacy and acting. Also known as Dionysus.

Beroe (*she who brings eggs*)   Semele's old nurse from Epidaurus. Juno uses her disguise to dupe Semele.

Cadmus (*from the East*)   brother of Europa, the King of Phoenicia and founder of Thebes. He and his wife Harmonia have four daughters: Autone, Ino, Agave and Semele; and one son, Polydorus.

Cenchreis   the wife of Cinyras, King of Assyria, and mother of Myrrha.

Ceres   (*grain*) daughter of Saturn and Rhea and sister of Juno and Jupiter. The goddess of the land – of its fertility, its ploughing, sowing and reaping.

Cephisus (*river of gardens*)   the river god who begets Narcissus with the nymph Liriope. The river is in central Greece.

CINYRAS (*plaintive cry*)   King of Assyria and Cyprus, son of Paphos and grandson of Pygmalion. He commits incest with his daughter Myrrha and thereby fathers Adonis. Cinyras had introduced the cult of Venus to Cyprus. He also establishes copper mining and sacred prostitution.

Cupid (*desire*)   god of love, son of Venus.

Danae   mother of Perseus, fathered by Jupiter who appears to Danae as a shower of gold.

Dictys (*net*)   a Lydian sailor.

ECHO a wood nymph in love with Narcissus. She can only repeat another's words because she has been punished for having distracted Juno with long stories while Jupiter had his way with the nymphs. Echo loves Narcissus unrequitedly and pines away.

Europa (*broad face*) daughter of the Phoenician King Agenor, brother of Cadmus. In the guise of a bull, Jupiter sweeps her off her feet. They have three sons. When she dies, the bull becomes a constellation in the heavens to honour Europa.

Fortune (*she who turns the year*) mistress of Time's wheel.

Furies or the three Erinnyes (*angry ones*). The avenging demons of the Underworld. They can pull their victims through the Earth to Hades.

Graces or the three Fates: Clotha (*spinner*), Lacheis (*measurer*), Atrops (*she who can neither be turned nor avoided*). They are the personification of grace and beauty who spread the joy of nature and influence artistic and imaginative works. Attendants to Venus.

Haemon (*skilful, bloody*) husband and brother of Rhodope with whom he is transformed into the mountain range Haemus in Thrace as a punishment for generating a cult to themselves as rulers of Thrace, in which they adopt the names of Juno and Jupiter.

HERMAPHRODITUS son of Mercury (Hermes) and Venus (Aphrodite). Brought up by the nymphs of Phrygia. When Salmacis' wish to be inextricably entwined with him is granted by the gods, his wish that any man who subsequently bathes in their fateful pool should lose his virility, is reciprocated.

Hymen the god of weddings – carries a torch and wears a veil, hence the traditional nuptial veil of the bride and the nomenclature of the virginal hymen membrane.

INO (*sinewy*) daughter of Cadmus and sister of Semele, Autone and Agave. The second wife of Athamas. After the death of her sister Semele, Ino persuades Athamas to welcome her nephew Bacchus and to raise him with their children. Juno, however, becomes angry because they have accepted the son (twice-)born of the adulterous affair between Jupiter and Semele. As a punishment, Juno makes both Athamas and Ino go insane. During the Bacchante revels, Ino joins her sisters in tearing limb from limb her nephew Pentheus. Eventually, Ino is transformed into the white goddess of sea spray and she guides sailors in storms.

ITYS (*willow*) child of Tereus and Procne. Killed by his mother who cooks his flesh as a feast for his father in order to avenge the rape of his aunt Philomela by his father.

JUNO daughter of Saturn and Rhea, the wife and sister of Jupiter, mother of Mars. The protector of women – particularly those who are married. Every woman has her Juno, a divine double which personifies and protects her femininity. The Matronalia is a festival given in her honour to re-establish harmony between man and woman. Juno is constantly battling in her relationship with husband and brother Jupiter, remaining faithful to him despite his constant infidelities. The peacock is her sacred bird.

JUPITER (or Jove) son of Saturn and Rhea, husband and brother of Juno. The god of sky, of daylight, of the weather – particularly of thunder and lightning. The supreme power, the President of the Council of gods, the source of all authority. Oaks are scared to Jupiter. He is an insatiable pursuer of nymphs – a cause of marital discord with Juno.

Leda (*lady*)   she hatches an egg bearing Helen of Troy. She conceived the child with Jupiter who came to her disguised as a swan.

Liriope (*lily face*)   a swarthy nymph of the fountain who is ravished by the river god Cephisus and gives birth to Narcissus.

Lycabus   a sailor.

Mars   Juno conceives Mars without Jupiter's aid, using a flower with fertile properties which Flora obtains for her. The god of war. He fathers two children: Romulus and Remus.

Medon   a sailor.

MIDAS (*seed*)   King of Phrygia. In infancy a procession of ants is observed carrying grains of wheat up the side of his cradle, placing them between his lips as he sleeps. Soothsayers say this presages the great wealth that will come to Midas. But the wish Bacchus grants Midas, as thanks for respecting Bacchus' childhood mentor, Silenus, brings no wealth and betrays a poverty of spirit. Midas becomes a devotee of Pan.

MINERVA   daughter of Jupiter. He swallows her mother Metis when it is revealed that any son born of their union will overthrow him as he overthrew his own father, Saturn. Minerva is born out of Jupiter's head(ache).

The goddess of arts and sciences who presides over intellectual and, in particular, academic activity.

MYRRHA (*bitter*)   with the help of her nurse, Myrrha tricks her father King Cinyras into incest and conceives Adonis. The gods change her into a myrrh tree (the resin of which is an aphrodisiac) which later bursts open allowing her child Adonis to be born.

NARCISSUS (*benumbing narcotic, a flower*)   the son of the river god Cephisus and the nymph Liriope. Narcissus has a stubborn pride in his own beauty and is indifferent to the passions of all. He falls hopelessly in love with his own reflection.

Nemesis (*due enactment, divine vengeance*)   the moon goddess who punishes crime, curbs excess, corrects wrongs.

NYMPHS   every river has a divine personality – every stream, brook, spring and pool harbours a divinity known as a nymph. They are not quite immortal: Plutarch estimated that the average lifespan did not exceed 9,620 years, but their privilege is always to remain young and beautiful. Their nourishment? Ambrosia. Their idle hours are spent spinning, singing, swimming. They occupy a similar place in ancient folklore to mermaids – sirens distracting and detroying men, and tempting gods. Naiads are nymphs specifically associated with fresh water. Dryads are tree nymphs. Oneddes are nymphs of mountains and grottos.

Opheltes   a sailor.

PAN (*pasture, all*)   fathered by Mercury. Said to be so ugly at birth that his mother, a nymph, ran away from him in fear. He is easy-going, lazy, loving nothing better than his afternoon nap. He lives in Arcadia and helps hunters find their prey. Yet the Arcadians pay him so little respect that, after a long day's hunting, they dart him with arrows for sport. Half man, half goat – a faun – with a crown of pine leaves, and a pipe made from the marsh reeds the nymph Syrinx changes into to avoid his clutches. The disreputable god of shepherds and flocks, woods and music. Likes the nymphs and boys – or, if unsuccessful with either, playing with himself. He's present in our modern word panic.

PANDION (*priest of the Jove festival*) King of Athens. Marries his maternal aunt and has four children by her: Erechtheus, Butes, Procne and Philomela. Arranges the marriage of Procne to King Tereus of Thrace in exchange for Tereus' assistance in fighting the Thebans. Pandion dies of grief when he learns what has befallen Procne, Philomela and his grandson Itys.

PENTHEUS (*pent-up grief*) son of Echion and Agave, grandson of Cadmus, cousin of Bacchus. The King of Thebes, after Cadmus abdicated reponsibility to him. He tries to prevent the spread of the Bacchant cult, but is eventually drawn by the Bacchante revels to Mount Cithaeron where he is attacked and killed by his mother Agave who tears off his head. His aunts and other women tear him limb from limb. This myth fuelled the Bacchae plays of Aeschylus and Euripides.

PHILOMELA (*sweet melody*) daughter of Pandion, sister of Procne and sister-in-law of Tereus, by whom she is raped and mutilated.

Pephos son of Pygmalion, father of Cinyras.

PROCNE (*the elder*)   the daughter of Pandion, sister of Philomela and wife of Tereus. To revenge her sister's rape and mutilation by her husband Tereus, Procne murders their son Itys and cooks him for Tereus to eat.

Proteus   a sailor.

Rhodope   daughter of the river god Strymon and the wife and sister of Haemon, with whom she is transformed into the mountain range in Thrace as a punishment for generating a cult to themselves as rulers of Thrace, in which they adopted the names of Juno and Jupiter.

SALMACIS   the nymph besotted by Hermaphroditus.

Saturn   the son of heaven and earth and the father of Jupiter and Juno. His son Jupiter, however, dethrones him and hurls him from Mount Olympus. Saturn then establishes himself on the Capitol (the future site of Rome). During the Saturnalia, the end-of-the-year festivals in honour of the god, the social order is inverted: slaves give orders to their masters, the masters perform the slaves' bidding.

SEMELE (*moon*)   daughter of Cadmus and Harmonia, and sister of Autone, Ino and Agave. Loved by Jupiter (their secret affair conducted in moonlight, revenged by Juno) and by him conceives Bacchus.

Silenus (*moon-man*)   an old, ugly satyr, very fat and always drunk. He raises Bacchus and remains his constant companion. Exceptionally wise, but he has to be forced to reveal his wisdom to men.

Syrinx (*reed*)   a beautiful and chaste nymph pursued by Pan. To escape his clutches, she transforms into marsh reeds on the banks of the River Ladon, only to be plucked up by Pan who binds them into his pipes.

TEREUS (*watcher*) son of Mars and husband of Procne. King of Thrace. He abducts and rapes his sister-in-law Philomela, and is then punished by both Procne and the gods by feasting on his son Itys.

TIRESIAS (*he who delights in signs*) son of Everes and the nymph Chariclo (companion of Minerva). A Theban prophet, a soothsayer, a seer. Struck blind by Juno, and in compensation given the gift of prophecy by Jupiter as well as the privilege of living for seven human generations – although Tiresias was a common title for soothsayers. He is attributed with disclosing the incest and patri-regicide of which Oedipus is unwittingly guilty; advising Pentheus not to oppose the cult of Bacchus; revealing the fate of Echo after her metamorphosis; predicting the fate of Narcissus.

TMOLUS the mountain in Phrygia called upon to judge between Pan's and Apollo's music.

Sources: Ovid, Hughes, Robert Graves' *The Greek Myths, The New Larousse Encyclopaedia of Mythology, The Penguin Dictionary of Classical Mythology, The Wordsworth Classical Dictionary*, Carlos Parada's *Genealogical Guide to Greek Mythology.*

Metamorphoses

A SELECTION OF OTHER TRANSLATIONS

Although many of Ovid's tales would not necessarily
have been the source of the myths, they would have been
the chief conduit – especially for Chaucer and the
Renaissance writers. Shakespeare, Marlowe, Jonson and
so on all made direct translations from Ovid as well as
adapting his material to their own ends. The following
selection of poetic and dramatic responses to Ovid's
'Metamorphoses' relate specifically to the tales we have
adapted for the theatre.

'Though I see many excellent thoughts in Seneca, yet he
of them who had a genius most proper for the stage was
Ovid. He had a way of writing so fit to stir up a pleasing
admiration and concernment, which are the objects of a
tragedy, and to show the various movements of a soul
combating betwixt two different passions, that, had he
lived in our age, or in his own could have writ with our
advantages, no man but must have yielded to him.'

> John Dryden, Poet Laureate,
> 'Of Dramatic Poesy: An Essay', 1668

Midas Let it be gold Bacchus.
Bacchus Midas, thy wish cleaveth to thy last word.
Midas Tush, he is a drunken god, else he would not
   have given so great a gift.

> from 'Midas', a play by John Lyly, 1591

Midas Alas! I cannot bite! as it approached
  I felt its fragrance, thought it would be mine,
  But by the touch of my life-killing lips
  'Tis changed from a sweet fruit to tasteless gold.
  Bacchus will not refresh me by his gifts,
  The liquid wine congeals and flies my taste.
  Go, miserable slaves! Oh, wretched king!
  Away with food! Its sight now makes me sick.
  Bring in my couch! I will sleep off my care,
  And when I awake I'll coin some remedy.
  I dare not bathe this sultry day, for fear
  I be enclosed in gold. Begone!
  I will to rest: – Oh, miserable king!

from Mary Wollstonecraft Shelley,
'Midas: A Drama in Two Acts', 1820

'Myrrha was joyed the welcome News to hear;
But clogged with Guilt, the Joy was unsincere:
So various, so discordant is the Mind,
That in our Will, a different Will we find.
Ill she presaged, and yet pursued her Lust;
For guilty Pleasures give a double Gust.'

from 'Cinyras and Myrrha', John Dryden, 1700

' . . . Thereus became a lapwynch, whych is a fowl byrde
and a vylaynous for the trayson that he hade don to the
damoyselle Phylomena. Prone becam a swalowe, and
Phylomena became a nyghtyngale. Yet her songe cryeth
out vpon alle vntrue lovers, and sayth that they shal be
destroyed And for bycause she hateth them, she syngeth
the moost swetly that she can whan the prymtemps is
comen in the buscage, occy, occy, occy.'

from 'The Booke Intituled Ovyde of Methamorphoseos',
translated and printed by William Caxton, 1480

Marcus Fair Philomel, why, she but lost her tongue,
  And in a tedious sampler sewed her mind:
  But, lovely niece, that mean is cut from thee;
  A craftier Tereus, cousin, hast thou met,
  And he hath cut those pretty fingers off,
  That could have better sewed than Philomel.   *(II,iv)*

Titus Lucius, what book is that she tosseth so?
Lucius Grandsire, 'tis Ovid's Metamorphosis;
  My mother gave it me. . .
Titus Soft, so busily she turns the leaves!
  Help her: what would she find? Lavinia, shall I read?
  This is the tragic tale of Philomel,
  And treats of Tereus' treason and his rape;
  And rape, I fear, was root of thy annoy'   *(IV,i)*
              from 'Titus Andronicus', Shakespeare, 1589

'And every smile doth send his own again
This cheers him, but he cannot hear a sound
Break from the watery prison, and he then
Complains a fresh, that his unhappy wound
      Admits no cure, and as he beats his breast,
      The Conflict under water is expressed.'
              from 'Narcissus or the Self-Lover',
                        James Shirley, 1646

' . . . She used in this light rayment as she was,
To spread her body on the dewy grass:
Sometimes by her own fountain as she walks,
She nips the flowers from off the fertile stalks,
And with a garland of the sweating vine,
Sometimes she doth her beauteous front in-twine:
But she was gathering flowers with her white hand,
When she beheld Hermaphroditus stand

By her clear fountain, wondering at the sight,
That there was any brook could be so bright:
For this was the bright river where the boy
Did die himself, that he could not enjoy
Himself in pleasure, nor could taste the blisses
Of his own melting and delicious kisses . . . '

from 'Salmacis and Hermaphroditus',
Francis Beaumont, 1602

'Now have I brought a work to end which neither
    Jove's fierce wrath,
Nor sword, nor fire, nor fretting age with all the force
    it hath
Are able to abolish quite. Let come that fatal hour
Which (saving of this brittle flesh) hath over me no
    power,
And at his pleasure make an end of my uncertain time.
Yet shall the better part of me assured be to climb
Aloft above the starry sky. And all the world shall never
Be able for to quench my name. For look how far so ever
The Roman Empire by the right of conquest shall extend,
So far shall all folk read this work. And time without
    all end
(If poets as by prophecy about the truth may aim)
My life shall everlasting be lengthened still by fame.'

Closing lines of the last book (XV) of Ovid's
'Metamorphoses', translated by Arthur Golding, 1567 –
the translation used by Shakespeare and his
contemporaries.

Acknowledgements

Research material was compiled with the assistance
of Emily Kline. Additional contributions came from
Simon Sinfield, Tim Sheader, Melly Still, Alison Reid,
Sam Dastor and the original RSC ensemble, and Cheryl
Farney. Thanks are also due to Alastair Macaulay for
guidance. Special thanks to John Cannon and Maggie
Lunn (casting), Denise Wood (Producer) and Adrian
Noble.

SR/TS

Drafted by Tim Sheader; cartography by Nigel Lee

Euxine
(Black Sea)

Byzantium or
Constantinople (Istanbul)
Propontis
(Sea of Marmora)
PROCONNESUS

PHRYGIA

•Troy
TROAS (THE TROAD)

LESBOS

•Phocaea
LYDIA / MAEONIA
(TURKEY)
•Sardis
River Pactolus
HIOS
Hypaepa   Mount
Tmolus

SAMOS

ICARIA

OS

NAXOS

IOS   COS

RHODES

ASSYRIA
(SYRIA)

CYPRUS
Paphos

(LEBANON)

Cyrenic Sea
(Mediterranean Sea)

(JORDAN)

(ISRAEL)

River Nile

ARABIA
(SAUDI ARABIA)

(EGYPT)

Arabian Gulf
(Red Sea)   •Sabea